Offerings from Adelynrood's Kitchen

Recipes for Sharing

Adam Segal

Chef Manager
Adelynrood Retreat and Conference Center
Byfield, MA

Acknowledgements

With special thanks to Carolyn Shilling Gill, whose leadership inspired me to create, to connect, and to excel. A team of sharp-eyed copy editors led by Nancy Lowry made this book legible. With her discerning eye and her generous heart, my fiancée, Linda Burke, helped me immeasurably on this project.

My heartfelt appreciation to all of those who contributed photographs and guided this book throughout its creation:

Lois Bennett, Joan Bowers, Mary Blount, Linda Burke, Susan Butler, Sharon Clark, Mimi Delcuze , Kay Evans, Carolyn Shilling Gill, Susan Gillespie , Carol Kingston, Nancy Lowry, Betty Mayben, James Otis Ostertag, Kathryn Ostertag, Diane Ruark , Judith Schwenk, Marion Sokolov, Louise Valleau, Susan Wasmer, Irma Wyman, and Margaret Young.

Our apologies if, despite our best efforts, we are remiss in including your contribution.

ISBN 978–0–615–80444–6

Design and Art Direction by Liz Gill Neilson
Illustrations by Margaret Young

Printed in The United States of America

www.adelynrood.org

CONTENTS

Preface · 6

Who We Are · 9

THE DAY BEGINS · **10**

WHEN THE LUNCH BELL RINGS · 16
Salads 18
Soups 41
Sandwiches, Etc. 50

OUR EVENING MEAL · **56**
Poultry 58
Seafood 69
Red Meat 71

SUNDRY SAVORIES · **76**

SENSIBLE SWEETS &
LAVISH INDULGENCES · **82**

Index · 110

PREFACE

There is something bewildering yet inviting about the early-morning Adelynrood kitchen. The dormant kitchen is unexpectedly silent, the air still chilly with just the smell of coffee brewing.

However, calm as it may be, the well-worn workspace abounds with potential. On my first visit to the Adelynrood kitchen, I was struck by its rustic, homey character. There are windows with a view and enough space never to feel cramped, a rarity in most commercial kitchens. Along with the sense of separation from the rest of the chaotic world, there was a feeling that pages of the calendar were flipping backwards to an earlier generation. Two thoughts crossed my mind: this place is something special, and meals for 80 or 90-- how hard can that be?

Now some years later, I realize that the first thought was spot on and the second turned out to be the naiveté of the new recruit. In fact, the challenges have never let up; if they had, I would be busy unearthing new challenges. The recipes offered in this book are the results of my years at Adelynrood listening to what our guests wanted, and from some gentle nudging to encourage them to stretch their comfort level with something unfamiliar. Not every meal needs to be a challenge; nonetheless, it can still be like

an unopened book with new worlds inside. A typical day might begin with recipes from New England, continue with a lunch of Asian-themed salads, and conclude in the evening with a stew from Greece. We are fortunate enough to choose among a bounty of foods rushed to us from all over the planet, and I think it befits us to draw out our culinary imaginations.

From the first meal I served here, it has been my goal to offer healthy, interesting meals, made entirely from scratch. There are easier ways to cook but none as satisfying. My style is to bring an eclectic, cross-cultural range of foods loaded with fresh vegetables and bold flavors that are as attractive to the eyes as they are to the palate. Accommodating personal palates means more than just serving dishes with foreign names. One group of guests wants to simplify with the lean and well-composed salads that a health spa might serve. Another group expects carefully prepared "meat and potatoes." Fortunately for our kitchen, there is also an accommodating, in-between group of diners who are delighted to eat anything put in front of them, as long as they don't have to cook and clean up. The one thing that all of our guests (except the youngest ones) have in common is that they love their vegetables.

This book is filled with our most requested recipes during my years here; a compendium of "greatest hits" which have repeatedly proven their worth. The majority of our meals are served in the heat of summer, so we begin the book with a variety of cold salads. Meals for the cooler seasons are also easy to find. If you prefer meatloaf and Deep Dark Chocolate Bundt Cake, rather than a trout with charmoula sauce and a stuffed pear for dessert, there are recipes here for you. There is healthy, and there is indulgent. While some recipes may be unfamiliar, I have not neglected the comfort foods that induce sighs and repeat trips back to the buffet.

In the Adelynrood kitchen, we train plenty of new chefs and support staff every year. Working with the chefs, I have the advantage of gleaning their favorite recipes and learning from their styles and techniques. Our chefs corral a new group of variously-skilled workers in our seasonal kitchen each spring, and we train them to become competent and speedy prep cooks before the fall weather comes and it is time for them to return to school. With the help of all my staff, these recipes were born and tested on our very forgiving guests, then refined until we found the sweet and savory taste of success. Other recipes have been inspired by my favorite chefs and adapted to satisfy our most discerning diners.

There are those who take up a career in cooking because it is so gratifying to please an audience with what they crave. Few professions have the advantage of rewarding one's efforts with such immediate and sincere gratitude. There are also those who choose the culinary art for its intricacies of skills and timing. Like any artisan, that chef is constantly refining lessons learned in order to create his or her own style that evolves with the trends of the day. I think that even a more common motivation for one to choose to spend long days in a hot, windowless room is the group of cooks who fall into the trade by happenstance. There was a need for money, there was an opening in the kitchen, or a position to which to advance, and the manager simply said, "OK, there's your station, get to work!" I can honestly say that something of all three of these categories of chefs defines how I made my way to Adelynrood.

I began cooking mostly so I could eat what I wanted, and I hope that it made my mother's hardworking life a little easier as well. My first professional kitchen was in a meditation center, a great place to learn discipline. I moved on to cook for a university, to catering work, and to restaurants. I learned quickly that restaurant work was not for me. To work in restaurants is to flourish on unpredictability. It takes a certain personality that thrives on the adrenalin of a frantic dinner rush. Young cooks seem to love numbers and invariably work into their conversation the number of "covers" served during a meal period. If you're not careful, the cooking becomes more about numbers than about what and whom are being served. By the end of my shifts I would feel as though I had just sprinted to a distant finish line, while still needing to make sure I was prepared for the next day.

I loved working with food but was dismayed to find out that restaurant work did not agree with me. Fortunately, there are many ways to be a chef that do not involve restaurants. After I worked in professional kitchens for six years, my parents and stepfather recognized that my B.A. might not lead to my life's work. I was given the sage advice that I could advance my career more readily with formal training at a cooking school.

One goes to cooking school to learn the fundamentals of cooking. Experienced chefs know there is too much to learn all at once so they do their best to fill a young cook's head: the four ways to thicken a sauce and the five mother sauces; don't over proof your breads or sauté with wet meat; salt in the water for green vegetable blanching and salt and vinegar for poaching; honing the chef's knife; educating taste buds; learning to be efficient as if your life depended on it; how to know when a braise is done; the Italians who gave birth to classical cuisine and the French who organized it all; trim, trim, trim, and then learning to think about how to utilize every bit of trim and leftover; how to set prices on a menu; listening to your clientele; when to fire your entrée and when to fire your sous-chef; managing personality conflicts and learning that flexibility must be paramount —oh, and wash your hands again… please!

No one graduates from cooking school as a chef. It is the triumphs, failures, and lessons of putting it all into practice which form a chef. I kept on cooking eleven more years until I was ready for Adelynrood. They were good years to put into practice what I was learning, and to learn from what I failed to put into practice. In the end, a friend mentioned an ad for Adelynrood that he saw online, and I was hooked. On my best days, I see myself as very lucky to have stumbled into a career which encourages the creative artisan in me to satisfy and fill the rumbling bellies of diners.

The old expression is, "you are what you eat," but the truth is that we are far more than what we eat. As omnivores, human beings can survive and even thrive on the most astonishing varieties of food. A diet rich in whale blubber, or whose staple food is bananas, can also be healthy and fulfilling. It's not just food that brings us health; it is everything we imbibe--from the people we surround ourselves with, to the media we watch, to the generosity of our hearts. For chefs who obsess about food, it is important to remember that our diet is just one component of what nurtures us. For those with unused kitchens, I offer the reminder that cooking can also be a part of what nourishes us.

There are benefits to cooking beyond filling our bellies in a thrifty fashion. We cook to take control of our lives. In a world where we give up so many of our freedoms: our time, our boundaries, our creativity, how we show our love; cooking gives the opportunity to nourish our selves and others in some unexpected ways. Even cleaning up has its greater significance because we deal with waste and learn what to improve for the next time. We also get to practice not being entitled to having someone else serve us. In cleaning we maintain ourselves; we remember that work is work, no matter what the content. Work becomes loaded with negative connotations only when we decide to describe the tasks that way. Besides, it's a good time to get up and work off a few of those calories.

The cook is just one element of the intricate cornucopia that nourishes us. Long before the cook peels an onion, there is the market, the truck that brought it there, the farmer that grew it, the clouds that watered it, the seed that sprouted. Food alone is not enough to feed us. We feed our belly with food, feed our mind with knowledge, and feed our hearts with compassion. Someone once said that, "It's not just the food in front of us, but our readiness to receive… that allows the food to do its feeding." Cooking can inspire a humbleness that makes us ready to be fed. Part of the joy of this job is that I get to serve others while challenging myself creatively. The core of this job is not creating; it is serving, which is why I am a chef. In the end, this world needs more cooks and, possibly, fewer cookbooks. May this book encourage the server in you.

Adam Segal, *Chef Manager*
Adelynrood, April 2013

WHO WE ARE

THE SOCIETY of the Companions of the Holy Cross is composed of approximately eight hundred women, lay and ordained members of the Anglican Communion, called to live under a rule of intercessory prayer, thanksgiving, and simplicity of life. Companions pray and work with intentional concern for social justice, the unity of all God's people, and God's mission in the world. They practice peace and reconciliation, acknowledging responsibility for the environment and for economic justice in the world.

In 1915, Companions designed and supervised the building of Adelynrood, a large, shingled, summer retreat house in Byfield, Massachusetts. Each summer at Adelynrood, the Society offers silent retreats, quiet days, and study programs on spiritual, religious, educational, and social justice topics. In June, 2000, a new, year-round wing, St. Clare, opened to enable Companions to extend their ministry at Adelynrood beyond the summer season.

Menus at Adelynrood are designed to make the best use of what the season has to offer. Meals are made with fresh produce prepared in a simple fashion that accentuates the underlying natural flavors and reflects a variety of ethnic and regional cuisines.

Three times daily Companions and guests give thanks for the gifts of creation and for table partnership of beautifully prepared natural food accompanied by the joy of sharing it in the company of new and renewed friendships.

THE
DAY
BEGINS

Fresh Corn Griddle Cakes 12

Morning Glory Muffins 13

Distinctive Zucchini Walnut Bread 15

FRESH CORN GRIDDLE CAKES

Traditional American cuisine is blessed with all manner of cornbread. Alter the heating method and a few ingredients, and the bread you eat could be corn pone, dodgers, johnnycakes, ashcakes, or hoecakes (which are cooked on the flat side of a garden hoe). This version is closer to what we call pancakes. The Virginia woodsman, C.D. Spach, passed on this recipe. When the fresh corn is sweet and the maple syrup is real, this is my favorite pancake in the world. **Yields 12 to 14 griddle cakes.**

2-3 ears of fresh corn, shucked
1 cup all-purpose white flour
1 cup stone-ground cornmeal
1 tablespoon baking powder
1 tablespoon sugar
Pinch of salt
2 large eggs, beaten
¼ cup vegetable oil
1 cup buttermilk
Spray oil for pan coating

1. Stand an ear of corn at a 45 degree angle and scrape the corn off of the cob into a bowl with a sharp knife. Next, using the back edge of the knife, scrape the cob to extract the tasty "milk" from the cob.

2. Sift together the flour, cornmeal, baking powder, sugar, and salt. In a separate bowl mix the eggs, oil, buttermilk, and the corn kernels.

3. Mix the wet and dry ingredients. This batter tends to thicken quickly; you may need to add a little more buttermilk to thin it

4. Warm a large cast iron skillet over medium heat. Spray the pan with oil and spoon out four-inch pancakes. Flip the cakes when you see bubbles forming near the edges of the cakes. Serve hot with maple syrup and watch your guests smile at their good fortune.

"When the fresh corn is sweet, and the maple syrup is real, this is my favorite pancake in the world."

Pam's Morning Glory Muffins

I love a muffin with texture that lets you know that you are not just eating cake batter cooked in the shape of a cupcake. Chef Pam McKinstry, who created these muffins in 1978 for her Morning Glory cafe on Nantucket Island, seemed to revel in tossing together a hodgepodge of "let's clean out the refrigerator" ingredients. But the flavors blend beautifully and the muffin has become a classic. Some say these muffins actually taste better a day after baking when the flavors have melded. Our own Chef, Pam Tardiff, first brought these to our kitchen. They can be stored at room temperature, if covered for up to 3 days, or you can freeze them for up to 2 months..

Yields 16 muffins.

1¼ cups sugar
2¼ cups unbleached all-purpose flour
1 tablespoon ground cinnamon
¼ teaspoon nutmeg
2 teaspoons baking soda
½ teaspoon salt
½ cup coconut, shredded and sweetened
¾ cup raisins
1 large apple, peeled and grated
1 cup crushed pineapple, drained
2 cups grated carrots
½ cup coarsely chopped pecans or walnuts
3 large eggs
1 cup vegetable oil
1½ teaspoon pure vanilla extract

1. Position a rack in the lower third of the oven and preheat to 350 degrees. Prepare muffin tins with oil or paper muffin cups.

2. Sift or whisk together the sugar, flour, cinnamon, nutmeg, baking soda, and salt into a large bowl. Add the coconut, raisins, apple, pineapple, carrots, and nuts, and stir to combine.

3. In a separate bowl, whisk the eggs with the oil and vanilla. Pour into the bowl with the dry ingredients and blend well.

4. Spoon the batter into muffin tins, filling each to the brim. Bake for 35 minutes or until a toothpick inserted into the middle comes out clean. Cool muffins in the pan for 10 minutes, then turn out onto a rack to finish cooling.

DISTINCTIVE ZUCCHINI WALNUT BREAD

What could be distinctive about this old standby that comes to the rescue whenever the squash plants seem inexhaustible? Simply stated— this version is the best. We started with Sabrina Henderson's Bon Appétit *recipe and noticed how we could make this temptation healthier and even better tasting. The result is delicious, stores beautifully, and is a nice alternative to richer versions that can be traitorous to one's diet.*

Yields two 8 x 4 x 2 ½-inch loaf pans.

2 cups coarsely grated zucchini (about 2 medium sized)
1½ cups all-purpose flour
½ cup whole-wheat flour
2 teaspoons ground cinnamon
1 teaspoon salt
1 teaspoon baking soda
1 teaspoon ground allspice
½ teaspoon baking powder
¾ cup white sugar
¾ cup light brown sugar
¼ cup honey
1 cup vegetable oil
3 large eggs
1 tablespoon vanilla extract
2 teaspoons grated lemon peel
1 cup walnuts, toasted and coarsely chopped (about 4 ounces)

1. Preheat oven to 325 degrees. Butter and flour the two loaf pans.

2. Squeeze the grated zucchini in small fistfuls to get rid of excess liquid.

3. Whisk flours, cinnamon, salt, baking soda, allspice, and baking powder in medium bowl to blend.

4. Whisk sugars, honey, vegetable oil, eggs, vanilla, and lemon peel in large bowl to blend.

5. Whisk in flour mixture. Mix in zucchini and walnuts. Pour batter into prepared pans.

6. Bake breads until tester inserted into center comes out clean, about 1 hour 15 minutes. Let stand 10 minutes. Turn breads out onto rack and cool completely. This can be made 1 day ahead. May be stored at room temperature or frozen if wrapped well once it has cooled.

When the
Lunch Bell Rings

SALADS

Cancun Shrimp, Avocado & Corn Salad 18

Chapel Garden Salad 19

Chicken Salad in the Spanish Style 20

Curry Barley Salad 21

Festive Rice Salad 22

Gentle Gigandes: A Bean Salad 24

Gezer Chai: Moroccan Carrot Salad 25

Harvest Couscous Salad 26

Kalamatta Spaghetti 29

Orzo Salad with Chinese Accent 30

Roast Beet & Watermelon Salad 32

Roast Sweet Potato Crunch Salad 33

Summer Delight Chinese Noodle Salad 35

Sweet Corn Salad with Buttermilk Dressing 36

Tuscan Potato Salad 38

Wild Waldorf with a Twist 40

SOUPS

Luscious Lentil Soup with Kale 41

Crimson Plum Soup 42

Emerald Gazpacho 43

Fresh Chili Chicken Chili 44

Chicken Soup, Vietnamese-Style 47

Potato Leek Soup Goes Green 48

SANDWICHES, ETC.

Cheddar, Pear and Ham Sandwich 50

Pissaladière: A French Pizza 52

Spinach Pie with Feta & Dill 54

Turkey Mushroom Burger 55

CANCUN SHRIMP, AVOCADO & CORN SALAD

Cilantro and lime lend a Southwestern flair to this enticing entree salad. We have served this as a sandwich, or in little nests of Boston lettuce, or as a stuffing in a halved avocado. All are delicious. Any size shrimp will work for this salad, but avoid the often flavorless precooked shrimp. Larger shrimp should be cut into bean-size morsels. Adding diced avocado to the mixture enhances the salad, but will shorten its shelf life to only one day.
Yields 6 servings.

1 large ear of corn, husked
1½ cups peeled small shrimp (try 60-70 count
   if available, about 10 ounces)
7 slices of bacon, cooked until crispy and crumbled
1 cup diced red bell pepper
2 tablespoons chopped fresh cilantro
2 tablespoons finely chopped green onion
4 teaspoons fresh lime juice
1 teaspoon grated lime peel
¼ teaspoon hot pepper sauce or
   ½ teaspoon Old Bay seasoning blend
2 tablespoons mayonnaise
1-3 ripe avocadoes (optional use: 1 avocado
   if dicing, 3 avocadoes if stuffing)
Salt and pepper to taste
10 finger rolls cut horizontally in half (if using)

1. Bring several quarts of water to a boil.

2. Scrape the kernels off the corn. Place the corn in a strainer and blanch for 30 seconds in the boiling water. Dump the corn into a bowl of cold water to stop the cooking process.

3. Blanch the shrimp in the same boiling water for 60 to 90 seconds, depending on the size of the shrimp. Remove the shrimp and add them to the cold water with the corn. Drain when cool.

4. Add crumbled bacon, bell pepper, cilantro, green onion, lime juice, lime peel, and hot pepper sauce to the shrimp and corn mixture. Toss to blend.

5. Add mayonnaise, salt, and pepper to taste. If adding diced avocado, add it just before serving.

6. Depending on how you choose to serve this, add the chilled salad to halved avocadoes, to large finger rolls, or on top of a bed of lettuce. This salad can be made up to one day ahead without the diced avocado. Chill.

Chapel Garden Salad

"We must live from the work of our hands," said the Benedictine monk who inspired this recipe, Brother Victor-Antoine d'Avila-Latourrette. His French roots are evident in his classic preparations of earthy, yet refined salads. Those of us in the New World tend to forget that tuna can be the flavorful highlight of a well-balanced, attractive salad that doesn't contain a bit of mayonnaise. With good bread, this salad is enough for a complete meal. As long as you don't dress the salad or cut the avocado, it is fine to assemble this a day ahead, then cover and refrigerate. **Yields 6 to 8 portions.**

For the Salad

½ teaspoon salt
10 stalks of asparagus, tough ends removed, cut into 3inch pieces
1 cup red onion, cut in half and thinly sliced
1 large bunch spinach or 8 ounces baby spinach
1 six-ounce can of quality tuna, well drained and broken up
3 medium-sized ripe tomatoes, cut into wedges
8 white mushrooms, thinly sliced
2 ripe but firm avocados, scooped and sliced
3 hard boiled eggs, peeled and sliced

To Make the Dressing

¼ cup fresh lemon juice
1 tablespoon prepared chili sauce
1 teaspoon Dijon mustard
1 teaspoon prepared horseradish
1 garlic clove, minced
Pinch of paprika
Salt and freshly ground pepper to taste
⅓ cup extra virgin olive oil

1. Bring 3 quarts of water to a boil in a wide stockpot. Add ½ teaspoon of salt to help keep the asparagus green. Place the asparagus in a strainer and immerse the strainer into the boiling water for about 60 seconds. Remove the asparagus and quickly chill it in a bowl of cold water. Do the same with the red onions but cook them for no more than 5 seconds. Add the blanched onions to the cold water with the asparagus. Once cool, drain the asparagus and onions well.

2. Mix together all the dressing ingredients except the oil. Slowly whisk in the extra virgin olive oil. For a "creamier" dressing, mix all ingredients in a blender or food processor while adding the oil slowly.

3. Wash and dry the spinach. If using large leaf spinach it is best to remove the tough stems and rip the leaves into bite size pieces.

4. To assemble the salad, gently toss together the spinach, tuna, asparagus, red onion, tomato wedges, and mushrooms with the salad dressing. Garnish the salad with avocado slices and the sliced eggs.

CHICKEN SALAD IN THE SPANISH STYLE

Chicken salad can be juicy and full of flavor without mayonnaise. This recipe makes excellent use of a vinaigrette along with zesty olives and capers to elevate the flavors. To save a bit of time, try purchasing a fully cooked supermarket rotisserie chicken, and pull the meat from it. I love serving this over a bed of spinach with bread offered on the side and fresh tabouli. Cook's Illustrated *magazine penned the concept from which this recipe was derived.* **Yields 6 servings.**

2 pounds boneless, raw chicken breasts
Salt and pepper to taste

THE DRESSING
½ cup extra virgin olive oil
3 tablespoons sherry vinegar (or balsamic)
⅔ cup of jarred roasted red peppers, rinsed.
1 small clove garlic, minced
2 teaspoons any brown mustard

THE SALAD
1 small shallot, minced (about 2 tablespoons)
3 tablespoons minced fresh parsley leaves
1¼ cups celery, very thinly sliced (about 2 ribs)
½ cup chopped green olives
2 tablespoons capers
⅔cup of jarred roasted red peppers, rinsed and cut the size of a thick matchstick
½ cup toasted and sliced almonds

1. Season the chicken with salt and pepper. Roast in a 375-degree oven until an instant-read thermometer inserted in the thickest part registers 160 to 165 degrees, about 35 minutes depending on the thickness of the meat. Let the meat cool to room temperature before shredding it or cutting it into 2" long shards.

2. Purée the olive oil, vinegar, ⅔ cup roasted red peppers, garlic, mustard, ¼ teaspoon salt, and ½ teaspoon pepper in blender until smooth. Transfer to bowl.

3. Add shallot, parsley, celery, olives, capers, and remaining ⅔ cup red peppers to vinaigrette; stir to combine. Add shredded chicken and toss gently to combine; let stand at room temperature 15 minutes. Adjust seasoning with salt and pepper, then sprinkle with almonds. Serve immediately.

Curried Barley Salad

Don't miss out on barley. It has an appealing chewy texture complemented by a slightly nutty taste, and lots of good dietary fiber. Pearl barley cooks quickly and is a great alternative to rice. Here we combine the barley with carrots, edamame (shelled soy beans), and blanched red cabbage. This satisfying salad is a vibrantly colorful cross-cultural fusion that makes a great accompaniment to the Cheddar, Pear and Ham Sandwich.
Yields 6 portions as a side salad.

1 tablespoon canola oil
1 small onion, finely diced
1 teaspoon curry powder
½ teaspoon salt for the barley cooking water
⅓ cup uncooked pearl barley
1 cup cold water to cook barley
1 cup red cabbage, sliced in thin two inch pieces

Pickling Brine
¼ cup red wine vinegar plus 1½ cup water
2 tablespoons sugar
½ teaspoon salt

The Dressing
4 ounces pineapple juice
1 tablespoon vegetable oil
1 tablespoon honey
1 tablespoon white vinegar
½ lemon, juiced
1 teaspoon grated or minced fresh ginger
¾ teaspoon salt
¼ teaspoon pepper

Add before serving:
½ cup frozen shelled edamame (soy) beans, thawed
¼ cup carrot, shredded or, even better,
    cut in a fine julienne

1. Heat a medium sauté pan to mid heat and add the oil. When the oil begins to shimmer, add the diced onions and cook for about 3 minutes, stirring occasionally. Add the curry powder and salt and continue to stir for another minute. Add the uncooked dry barley. Stir, then add water. Bring to a boil, then simmer covered on low heat for about 30 minutes. Let the barley sit covered without heat for a final 5 minutes. Cool the barley by emptying it out onto a cookie tin.

2. Bring 6 cups of water to a boil. Blanch the cabbage for one minute until crisp-tender then quickly remove and rinse with cold water to stop the cooking process.

3. After draining the cabbage, add the vinegar, water, sugar, and salt to the cabbage. Let the cabbage pickle in this mixture for at least a half hour before rinsing and draining it. Discard the pickling brine.

4. Whisk all ingredients for the dressing together. Up to this point the salad can be made a day ahead.

5. Toss together the barley, the drained red cabbage, raw thawed edamame beans, and carrots. Add the dressing and serve.

FESTIVE RICE SALAD

A few simple things bring success to a pasta or rice salad. The proportion of vegetables to the rice or pasta is essential; I like lots of veggies to bring color, texture, and nutrition to a salad. The vegetables should be cut to complement the shape of the pasta or rice. Of course, a good quality dressing will be the first thing the diner tastes. Because the texture of the rice is so important, here the rice is cooked like a pasta so as to be sure not to over cook it. While the rice is still a little warm, some of the dressing is tossed with it so the flavors can soak in. The vegetables are cut tiny so as to appear almost like confetti when mixed with the rice. **Yields 12 portions as a side salad.**

1 cup long grain white rice
2 quarts boiling water
½ teaspoon salt

THE DRESSING
Zest of one lemon and two limes
Juice of one lemon and two limes
1 tablespoon diced shallot
½ teaspoon of salt
¼ teaspoon of pepper
⅓ cup extra virgin olive oil
⅓ cup vegetable oil (such as canola or corn)

THE VEGETABLES
½ cup red bell pepper, diced very small
½ cup yellow bell pepper, diced very small
1 cup zucchini, cut in quarters lengthwise, remove spongy interior with knife and dice very small
4 green onions, sliced very fine
½ cup parsley, leaves cut very fine
½ cup cilantro, leaves cut very fine

1. Rinse rice in a strainer under cold running water for 30 seconds. Soak the rice in cold water for 30 minutes. Bring 2 quarts of water to a boil in a pot over high heat. Add the salt and the rice, stir it once, and boil uncovered for about 10 minutes. Taste the rice; firm is best. Drain the rice.

2. Let the rice drain for 10 seconds, then return it to the pot, off the heat. Cover the pot and set it aside to allow the rice to steam for 10 minutes.

3. While the rice steams, prepare the dressing: mix the salt and pepper, the lemon, lime juice, and zest, and the shallots in a bowl. Gradually whisk in the olive and vegetable oils. Dressing should taste acidic.

4. Dump the rice onto a cookie tin for quick cooling and fluff with a fork. After about 10 minutes, toss the rice with half of the dressing. Set the rice aside.

5. When the rice comes to room temperature, toss with all of the chopped vegetables, the chopped greens, and the remaining dressing. Taste to check the seasoning.

6. Best served at room temperature or slightly chilled. Many other vegetables can be used in this recipe: green beans cut very short, fennel root and greens, shredded carrot, or even diced pineapple, mango, or coconut. The salad will last up to 3 days if refrigerated.

GENTLE GIGANDES: A BEAN SALAD

Bean salads can be an unexpected pleasure. High in protein and low in fat, this salad has earned praise from our guests and is worth your consideration. Not surprisingly, gigandes beans are gigantic. These Greek beans look like very large lima beans. If you can't find the gigandes, the large lima bean or the butter bean makes a good substitution. Unlike some beans that can be simmered without presoaking, it is best to soak these beans in salted water overnight to keep them from splitting open while cooking, then change the water (which helps reduce gassiness) and simmer slowly. This is a great accompaniment to the Spinach Pie with Feta. **Yields 10 portions as a side dish.**

1½ cup gigandes beans (or large lima beans), soaked overnight, then simmered until soft but not mushy

1 cup yellow onion, finely diced

2 tablespoons olive oil

6 cups green Swiss chard, washed, with the center ribbed removed and saved, and leaves cut into 1 inch squares

1½ cup of the center rib of the Swiss chard, thinly sliced

1¼ cup good quality diced smoked ham

THE DRESSING

¼ cup white wine vinegar

1 teaspoon Dijon mustard

3 tablespoons fresh dill, finely chopped

¾ teaspoon salt

¼ teaspoon fresh ground black pepper

¾ cup extra virgin olive oil

1. Soak the dry beans in enough cold salted, water to cover the beans by 4 inches. Soak for at least 4 hours or overnight. Drain the soaking water and add enough water to cover the beans. Bring to a boil, then turn heat down to a simmer and cook until the beans are soft but not mushy. Drain and chill the beans.

2. Add olive oil to a large sauté pan on medium heat. When the oil begins to shimmer, add the diced onions. Stir occasionally until onions are translucent. Add the Swiss chard stems and a minute later add the cut Swiss chard. Continue to cook until the chard has wilted, about 2 minutes. Set aside the pan.

3. To make the vinaigrette, combine the vinegar, Dijon mustard, dill, salt, and pepper. Slowly whisk in the extra virgin olive oil.

4. Gently mix the beans with the onion mixture, the ham, and the vinaigrette. This salad may be served at room temperature or chilled.

Gezer Chai: Moroccan Carrot Salad

Of the many varieties of carrot salad, I like the Moroccan style the best. There are cooked versions, but good sweet raw carrots do the job even better. If your grater has different sizes on it, use the smallest one (but not the one for hard cheeses). Make the lustrous orange color beam by serving the salad inside a quartered avocado with a few toasted walnuts on the side and a sprig of mint. Gil Marks' wonderful book, Olive Trees and Honey, *brought this vibrant dish to our kitchen.*

Yields 5 to 6 servings.

1 pound carrots, finely grated (about 4 cups)
1 red bell pepper, julienned in short thin pieces
¼ cup vegetable oil or extra-virgin olive oil
3 to 4 tablespoons fresh lemon juice
¼ cup chopped fresh cilantro or parsley
2 to 4 cloves garlic, mashed or minced
¼ teaspoon ground cinnamon
1 teaspoon sweet paprika
Pinch of salt
Chilies can be added to taste: either
   ½ teaspoon harissa (Northwest African chili paste)
   or 1 teaspoon minced jalapeño chilies.

1. In a large bowl, mix together all the ingredients.

2. Cover and let marinate in the refrigerator for at least 2 hours (this is essential) or up to 2 days to allow the flavors to meld and permeate the carrots.

3. Serve chilled or at room temperature. Optional garnishes: avocado, orange sections or toasted walnut.

Helpful Hint: *Make sure to marinate for at least 2 hours. I prefer a fine shred on the carrots. A small amount of red cabbage or julienned red bell pepper looks great. Optional garnishes: orange sections, toasted walnut.*

Harvest Couscous Salad

We eat with our eyes as well as our mouths, which must be why the throng of colors in this salad is so appealing. The fine grains of precooked couscous are familiar to most, but the larger caper-sized pearls of Israeli style couscous are an attractive alternative. This recipe cooks the couscous just like a pasta using two separate pots in order to give one pot its dandelion yellow color. After cooking the grains, this salad comes together quickly, will keep for several days, and is a noteworthy contribution to a picnic.

Yields 10 portions as a side salad.

½ cup wild rice
1 cup Israeli couscous, divided according to
   instructions
½ teaspoon salt for each pot of couscous
½ teaspoon turmeric
1 cup pecan pieces, chopped
½ cup dried apricots, sliced
2 ribs celery, sliced in half lengthwise,
   then thinly sliced
⅔ cup dried cranberries, rough chopped
4 scallions, thinly sliced

The Dressing
2 tablespoons red wine vinegar
1 tablespoon lemon juice
1 teaspoon Dijon mustard
1 teaspoon dried tarragon leaves
½ teaspoon table salt
⅛ teaspoon ground black pepper
½ cup extra virgin olive oil

1. Bring 2 cups of water to a boil. Add the wild rice and simmer on a low flame with a loose fitting lid for about 40 minutes. When done, empty the rice into a large mixing bowl so it will cool.

2. While the wild rice cooks, prepare the two pots of couscous. In the first pot, boil 4 cups of water with a ½ teaspoon of salt. Add 5 ounces of couscous and simmer on a low boil for 8 to 10 minutes. When the couscous has an al dente texture, drain it and rinse. Add the drained couscous to the wild rice.

3. Prepare the second pot of couscous identically to the first with one exception: add ½ teaspoon of turmeric to the water before adding the remaining 3 ounces of couscous.

4. To toast the pecans lay them out on a cookie tin and roast in a 350 degree oven until slightly darkened, about 5 to 7 minutes.

5. To make the dressing stir together the first six ingredients. Gradually whisk in the olive oil.

6. Add the cooled yellow couscous, the apricots, celery, cranberries, scallions, and pecans to the mixing bowl. Gradually pour on the dressing and thoroughly toss all the ingredients together. The salad will last up to three days if refrigerated.

KALAMATA SPAGHETTI SALAD

If boring pasta salad is what ails you, then take a trio of cured, intensely flavored accoutrements (like olives, capers, and anchovies) to give your pasta some backbone. This distinctive pasta dish, which has been adapted from The Olives Table *by Todd English, is delicious chilled, but I think that when served warm its robust flavors really dazzle. Can be made the day before and served with good results.*
Serves up to 6 as a side dish.

2 tablespoons olive oil
2 garlic cloves, thinly sliced
2 anchovy fillets, minced
1 tablespoon capers, chopped
1 cup pitted cured black olives, such as
    Kalamata, Gaeta, or oil-cured olives
½ teaspoon kosher salt
¼ to ½ teaspoon black pepper
1 tablespoon balsamic vinegar
½ pound spaghetti, broken into halves
1 tablespoon chopped fresh rosemary leaves
2 cup baby arugula, washed
½ cup scallions (about 1 ½ bunches),
    cut in fine rounds
1 cup grape tomatoes split in half
Shaved Parmesan cheese, for garnish

1. In a medium-size skillet over low to medium heat, add 1 tablespoon of the oil. Add the garlic, anchovy fillets, capers, and olives and cook until they are lightly toasted, about 5 to 7 minutes.

2. Transfer the olive mixture to a food processor or blender. While the machine is running, add the remaining tablespoon oil, the salt, pepper, and balsamic vinegar. Process until the mixture is completely smooth.

3. Bring a large pot of water to a boil over high heat and add the spaghetti. Cook until tender and drain.

4. While the pasta is still warm, add the olive paste and rosemary to the spaghetti. Toss well. Next mix in the arugula, scallions, and half of the grape tomatoes. Transfer the salad to a serving dish and conclude by garnishing with the remaining grape tomatoes. Serve with grated or shaved Parmesan cheese.

Orzo Salad with Chinese Accent

Or-zo-you think this is Asian, but it is really a cross-cultural fusion of Italian pasta and Chinese flavors. First described in the Moosewood Restaurant Low-Fat Favorites cookbook, this adapted recipe is a great accompaniment to an Asian-themed lunch like teriyaki salmon or scallion meatballs. If you are short on time, you may prepare steps 1 through 3 a day ahead.
Yields 8 portions as a side salad.

The Salad

2 teaspoons dark sesame oil
2 cups asparagus with-tough ends removed,
   cut on the diagonal into 1-inch pieces
¾ cup red bell pepper cut into ¼ inch diced pieces
   (about one large pepper)
One 15-ounce can Asian style baby corn,
   drained and rinsed, cut in half lengthwise
½ cup chopped celery
1½ cup shredded cabbage or any other
   finely shredded cabbage
1 cup frozen shelled edamame beans, thawed
5 scallions, thinly sliced on the diagonal
   (greens and white part)

The Dressing

3 tablespoons rice vinegar
3 tablespoons soy sauce
¼ teaspoon Chinese chili paste
   or pinch of cayenne
1 tablespoon grated or finely minced fresh ginger
2 cloves garlic, minced

1. Cook orzo in boiling, salted water until al dente, stirring frequently. Orzo cooks faster than most pasta; it's worth tasting it half way through its cooking. Drain, rinse with cold water, and transfer to a serving bowl. Toss with sesame oil.

2. Blanch asparagus in salted boiling water for about 2 minutes, until just tender. Drain and immediately submerge asparagus in cold water (to help maintain green color).

3. Add asparagus, bell peppers, baby corn, celery, shredded cabbage, edamame beans, and scallions to orzo.

4. Whisk together dressing ingredients and pour over orzo and veggies. Gently toss to coat and serve.

Roast Beet & Watermelon Salad

If one were to cook according to color, then the dazzling reds and purples of this salad would be on the top of my list of summer favorites. The unlikely combination of watermelon with beets and red onion harmonize together to make great music. It comes together beautifully and never fails to surprise our guests with its sweet and peppery combination of flavors. This dazzling salad is best enjoyed immediately.
Yields 6 servings.

4 golf ball size beets or 2 large beets
¼ cup red onion, very thinly sliced
8 red radishes, thinly sliced
2 cups seedless watermelon, cut into 1-inch cubes
1 cup red cabbage, sliced very thinly
20 basil leaves cut into julienne; if available
   use purple leaves or Thai basil
1 cup crumbled feta cheese

The Dressing
4 tablespoons raspberry or red wine vinegar
½ teaspoon Dijon mustard
1 teaspoon honey
6 tablespoons mild olive oil
Salt and freshly ground pepper to taste

1. Wrap beets in aluminum foil and roast in the middle of a 350 degree oven until beets can easily be pierced with a thin knife, about an hour depending on the size of the beet. Unwrap the beets and allow to cool.

2. Whisk all the dressing ingredients together in a bowl and taste to check the seasoning.

3. Once the beets are cool, slip off the skins, cut off the stems, and cut the beets into 1/4-inch slices.

4. Gently toss all salad ingredients together, except the feta cheese, then add the dressing and toss a bit more. Sprinkle the feta cheese on top.

Roast Sweet Potato Crunch Salad

This salad quickly became a favorite at Adelynrood. It puts on no airs and delivers a healthy combination of ingredients with a gratifying mix of textures and flavors. I've served it with American southern food, yet found that it complements many Asian lunches just as well. Roasting the potatoes (I prefer the red skinned sweet potatoes) best brings out their sweetness. Be careful when you roast the sweet potato chunks that they are tender but not mushy. In the unlikely case of leftovers, they will keep up to two days in the refrigerator. Thanks to Constance Snow's The Rustic Table *for the inspiration.*
Yields 7 servings as a side dish.

**2 pounds sweet potatoes, peeled and
 cut into ¾ inch chunks**
1 tablespoon vegetable oil
½ teaspoon salt tossed with the potatoes

The Dressing
2 tablespoons fresh lime juice
1 tablespoon finely grated fresh ginger
1 teaspoon honey
½ teaspoon dark or whole grain mustard
Pinch cayenne pepper
¼ teaspoon salt
3 tablespoons peanut oil

Garnish
¾ cup roasted unsalted peanuts, coarsely chopped
**½ cup finely diced sweet red bell peppers
 (about 1 red pepper)**
⅓ cup finely sliced scallions

1. Preheat the oven to 400 degrees.

2. Toss the sweet potatoes with the oil and salt. Spread the potatoes in a single layer onto a cookie sheet. Roast until the potatoes are lightly browned and tender, about 20-25 minutes. Allow the potatoes to cool to room temperature. We often roast the potatoes the day before completing the recipe.

3. To make the dressing, stir together the lime juice, ginger, honey, mustard, cayenne, and ¼ teaspoon of salt. Gradually whisk in the peanut oil until smooth.

4. Toss the cooled sweet potatoes in a bowl with the peanuts, bell peppers, scallions, and dressing. Let the salad sit at room temperature for at least an hour to let the flavors meld together.

Summer Delight Chinese Noodle Salad

*These Chinese noodles were a hit from the very first time they were served. The chilled noodles make a hearty main course and, for me, are an Asian comfort food that I never tire of. A tart and piquant dressing is essential to this dish. Because the ingredient list is a bit long we like to prepare the dressing the day before. To save a step, you could also purchase a precooked supermarket chicken and shred the meat for the salad. If fresh egg noodles are not available, you can substitute ¾ pound dried, thin, Chinese egg noodles or a thin pasta such as angel hair. Joyce Jue inspired this gratifying recipe that has served us well. **Yields 12 servings.***

The Dressing

¼ cup chunky peanut butter
1½ tablespoons sugar
1 teaspoon minced garlic
1 teaspoon finely grated fresh ginger
About ⅓ cup chicken stock or canned
   low-sodium broth or water
2½ tablespoons soy sauce
2 tablespoons peanut oil
4 tablespoons red wine vinegar
1½ teaspoons Asian sesame oil
½ teaspoon hot chili oil
½ teaspoon salt

For the Noodle Salad

2 medium Japanese eggplants
   or 1 large globe standard eggplant
2 tablespoons peanut oil
2 ounces snow peas, strings removed
1 pound fresh thin Chinese egg noodles
1½ teaspoons Asian sesame oil
1½ pounds of boneless, skinless chicken breast
1 medium scallion, thinly sliced
1½ cup canned roasted red bell pepper,
   rinsed and julienned
2 tablespoons toasted sesame seeds, preferably black
Generous handful of fresh cilantro leaves

1. Prepare the sesame dressing: Whip together all the ingredients in a bowl. If the dressing is too thick, stir in a little more chicken stock.

2. Preheat oven to 375 degrees. Slice the eggplants 1/2 inch thick and brush with the peanut oil. Bake for about 15 minutes or until the eggplant yields easily when depressed with your thumb. Bake the chicken breasts until they reach an internal temperature of 165 degrees. When the eggplant and the chicken have cooled, cut them into strips the size of your pinkie finger.

3. In a large, 4-quart saucepan of boiling, salted water, blanch the snow peas until they turn bright green, about 30 seconds. Using a slotted spoon, transfer to a bowl of cold water, then drain and pat dry.

4. Cut the raw noodles into 4- to 6-inch lengths. Add the noodles to the boiling water and stir to separate the strands. Cook over moderate heat until tender, according to package directions. Drain, rinse with cold water; drain again. Transfer to a bowl and toss with the sesame oil.

5. Add half of the shredded chicken, the scallion, snow peas, and half of the sesame seeds to the noodles. Pour on the dressing and toss to combine. Mound the noodles in a shallow serving bowl and scatter the eggplants, red pepper strips and the remaining chicken over the top. Sprinkle with the remaining sesame seeds and the cilantro. May be served chilled or at room temperature.

SWEET CORN SALAD with Buttermilk Dressing

Is it a sign of progress that science brings me sweet fresh corn amidst a New England winter? Some would scorn me for cooking so out of season, but I just love the balance of textures and flavors in this salad. Maybe it's because this recipe is reminiscent of summer that I have made it year round. It has crunchy sweet corn enhanced with a tart, herby dressing and fresh herbs that tame the saltiness of the feta cheese. Lighter than a potato salad, it is visually like a beam of sunlight decorating your plate. Sometimes fresh corn can be chewy. A 30-second dip of the kernels in boiling water should remedy the problem. The author, Creamtea, from the excellent blog, Food52, inspired this variation of the recipe. **Serves 6 as a side dish.**

THE SALAD

2 ¾ cup uncooked corn kernels (about 3 ears of corn)
1 cup cucumber, peeled and seeded, then diced
    to the size of raisins
1 red bell pepper, seeded, ribs removed, and diced
    the size of corn kernels
4 scallions, the whites only, sliced fine
2 tablespoons fresh dill, minced
¼ cup minced, fresh parsley
Crumbled feta cheese as a garnish
½ teaspoon smoked paprika as a top garnish

THE DRESSING

¼ cup buttermilk
⅔ cups plain European style thin yogurt, stirred
1 tablespoon white wine vinegar
1 teaspoon honey
3 tablespoons minced Vidalia or other sweet onion
1 small clove garlic, minced and mashed with
    a pinch of salt
¼ cup extra-virgin olive oil
Salt and freshly ground pepper to taste

1. To make the dressing, combine the buttermilk, yogurt, vinegar, honey, onion, and garlic. Whisk in the olive oil in a slow stream until emulsified. Season with freshly ground pepper and salt to taste.

2. In a large bowl, toss the corn kernels to separate them, and then add the cucumber, red pepper, scallions, dill, and parsley. Up to this point, the salad can be prepared the day ahead.

3. When ready to serve toss the salad with the dressing and garnish with the feta cheese and smoked paprika. Best served slightly chilled. Salad will fade quickly the second day after the dressing is added.

Tuscan Potato Salad

With all of the possibilities that potatoes have to offer, here is a creative diversion that shows off their potential. Too many potato salads make mayonnaise the principal flavor. This recipe does away with the creamy dressing that hides the vibrant colors and replaces it with intriguing Mediterranean flavors. Once the potatoes are cooked, this recipe lays them out on a flat pan, which helps cool the potatoes and allows them to be tossed without breaking. Mixing some of the vinegar mixture with the potatoes while they are still warm infuses the flavors with the cooked potatoes.
Yields 8 portions.

2 pounds red potatoes, scrubbed & sliced ¼ inch thick
2 teaspoons salt

The Dressing
3 tablespoons red wine vinegar
2 tablespoons water
2 garlic cloves, minced
1 teaspoon fresh rosemary, minced
½ teaspoon salt
¼ teaspoon pepper
2 teaspoons Dijon mustard
¼ cup extra-virgin olive oil

The Vegetables
½ cup thinly sliced celery
2 tablespoons finely chopped fresh parsley
¾ cup green beans, stemmed and cut in half
1 cup thinly sliced roasted red bell peppers from a jar
¼ cup sliced green olives
½ cup shredded Asiago cheese

1. Start the potatoes cooking in cold salted water that thoroughly covers the potatoes. When the pot reaches a boil, reduce the heat to medium and simmer until potatoes are tender but firm enough not to fall apart in a salad. Watch closely so they do not overcook.

2. While the potatoes simmer, whisk vinegar, water, garlic, rosemary, ½ teaspoon salt and ¼ teaspoon pepper in a bowl. Don't add the mustard or oil yet.

3. Remove the potatoes with a strainer. The same pot of water will be used to blanch the green beans. Spread the drained potatoes in an even layer on a rimmed baking sheet. Drizzle half of vinegar mixture over hot potatoes and let stand until cool, about 20 minutes.

4. Blanch the green beans in the salted, boiling water to desired doneness. Drain and rinse beans with cold water.

5. Stir mustard into remaining vinegar mixture, then slowly whisk in the oil.

6. Scatter celery, parsley, green beans, peppers, olives, and Asiago cheese evenly over potatoes. Transfer potato mixture to a mixing bowl and toss gently with remaining vinaigrette until combined. This salad can be refrigerated for up to two days.

Wild Waldorf with a Twist

How often does a salad get sung about in a Broadway musical? Cole Porter cited the Waldorf Salad in his 1934 musical, Anything Goes *("You're the Top... you're a Waldorf Salad..."), and it's still found on modern menus in many forms. My favorite part of the Waldorf salad has always been the balance of tart and sweet accompanied by the crunch of the toasted nuts. Here, I add the chewy texture and earthiness of wild rice and ditch the richness of mayonnaise for a citrus and spice dressing. Once the rices are cooked and cooled, this salad is quick to prepare. Because this healthier alternative can be prepared a day ahead and travels well, it makes a notable potluck contribution. Leftovers will keep up to 3 days.* **Yields 12 servings as a side dish.**

⅔ cup wild rice (about 2 cups cooked)
1 cup brown rice— preferably long grain
   (about 3 cups cooked)
1 large Granny Smith apple, peeled
3 tablespoons fresh lemon juice
1 bell pepper any color—seeded and diced
1 cup diced celery
⅓ cup grated carrot
½ cup thinly sliced green onions (whites and greens)
¼ cup currants or raisins
¼ cup dried cranberries
¼ cup toasted almonds, chopped, or slivered
   or toasted walnuts

The Dressing
½ cup orange juice
1 tablespoon pure maple syrup — or honey
1 teaspoon ground coriander
½ teaspoon ground cardamom
1 tablespoon canola oil or other vegetable oil

1. In a saucepan with a tight-fitting lid, soak the wild rice in 1 cup of hot water for 30 minutes. Add 1½ cups of water, bring to a boil, and then lower to a simmer, cover and cook for about 45 minutes, until the rice is tender.

2. To prepare the brown rice, bring 2 cups of water to boil using a saucepan with a tight fitting lid. Add ½ teaspoon of salt to the water and then add the raw rice. Lower the heat to a simmer, cover, and cook until all the water is absorbed, about 40 minutes. The rices will cool quicker by emptying out the pots onto a cookie tin.

3. While the rices cook, dice the apple and toss with the lemon juice in a large bowl. Add the peppers, celery, grated carrot, green onions, currants or raisins, dried cranberries, and almonds or walnuts and set aside.

4. To make the dressing, simply whisk together all of the dressing ingredients. Add the cooked rice and the dressing to the bowl and toss well to combine. Salad can be served chilled or at room temperature.

LUSCIOUS LENTIL SOUP WITH KALE

Transform your lentil soup from blah to exceptional. You may use the larger standard "American" brown lentils in this recipe, but the flavor just won't be as good. The small French green lentils, also known as lentilles du Puy, have a less "muddy" flavor that is superb. A little wine and tomato add some flavor backbone to this soup. This comforting soup improves with a day or two in the fridge and if accompanied with good bread, salad, and a wedge of cheese it becomes a satisfying meal. A tip of the hat to Cook's Illustrated *for helping me remember how good this soup can be.*
Yields 10 servings.

3 tablespoons olive oil

1 large onion, chopped finely, about 1 cup

3 carrots, peeled and cut in half moons, about 1½ cups

2 stalks celery, sliced

3 cloves garlic, minced

1 can (14½ ounces) diced tomatoes, drained

1 bay leaf

1 teaspoon minced fresh thyme leaves (or ½ teaspoon of dried thyme)

1 cup French green lentils, rinsed and picked through

2 teaspoons table salt

½ teaspoon ground black pepper

½ cup dry white wine

4 cups low-sodium chicken broth

2 cups water

3 cups of kale, stripped from the stem, shredded and cut into short pieces

2½ teaspoons balsamic vinegar

1. Heat a thick-bottomed stockpot or Dutch oven to medium-high heat. Add olive oil, then onion, carrots, and celery; cook, stirring occasionally, until vegetables begin to soften, about another 5 minutes. Add garlic and cook another minute. Stir in tomatoes, bay leaf, and thyme; cook 1 minute.

2. Stir in lentils, salt, and pepper; cover (this is important to do). Reduce heat to medium-low, and cook until vegetables have softened, about 8 to 10 minutes.

3. Uncover and increase heat to high; add wine and bring to a simmer. Add chicken broth and water and then bring to boil. Cover partially and reduce heat to low. Simmer until lentils are tender but still hold their shape, 30 to 35 minutes; discard bay leaf.

4. To thicken the consistency, use an immersion blender or potato masher to puree a small portion of the soup. Or even better, add several cups of the soup to a blender and puree. Add this puree back to the soup pot.

5. Add the chopped kale to the soup pot and simmer 5 minutes longer. With the heat off stir in the balsamic vinegar. Taste the soup and adjust the seasoning to your preference.

CRIMSON PLUM SOUP

This may be our simplest soup, yet among the best we serve. The color of the crimson plums charms the eyes and the silky smooth, chilled soup with its slight tartness will captivate your palate as well. Most any type of plums will work here as long as they are not overripe.
Yields 8 servings.

3 to 4 black peppercorns
2 large slices of fresh ginger
1 whole allspice berry
1 cinnamon stick, crushed, if necessary
6 cups of chopped, pitted, skin on, red plums
    (approximately 2 pounds)
3 cups cranberry juice, chilled
⅓ cup honey
Fresh lemon juice to taste
Low fat sour cream for garnish
2 tablespoons toasted slivered almonds for garnish

1. Using cheesecloth, make a sachet with the peppercorns, ginger, allspice and cinnamon and tie it with butcher's twine. A large tea ball will also work.

2. Combine the plums, cranberry juice, sachet, and honey in a soup pot. Bring to a simmer and cook until the plums are tender, about 20 minutes. Remove and discard the sachet.

3. Transfer soup mixture into a blender and purée. Blend soup for 45 seconds or until very smooth. Straining the soup through a fine strainer will give it a beautiful consistency.

4. Season to taste with the lemon juice. Chill the soup thoroughly for at least 4 and up to 24 hours.

5. Toast the almonds in a small skillet on medium heat. Stir constantly until they become fragrant and begin to turn color (about 3 minutes).

6. Serve in a chilled bowl, garnished with a dollop of sour cream and a scattering of toasted, slivered almonds.

Emerald Gazpacho

The comfort foods of summer draw from the garden. One particularly satisfying category that is often overlooked are the chilled soups. These have a healthy richness and intensity that are best appreciated in smaller portions. This reimagining of the traditional gazpacho reawakens the appetite when the heat of the day has stilled it. Preparing this soup a day ahead will allow the flavors to mingle and will ensure that it is served thoroughly chilled. This gem of a recipe was inspired by Lukins and Rosso in their classic book, The New Basics.

Yields 6 portions.

1 cup ripe honeydew melon
   or 1 cup green seedless grapes
1 ripe avocado, pitted and scooped
½ cup green bell peppers, coarsely chopped
¾ cup cucumbers, peeled and coarsely chopped
½ cup celery, coarsely chopped
½ cup scallions, coarsely chopped
1 lime zested plus 1 tablespoon fresh lime juice
2 tablespoons chopped fresh mint leaves
¼ cup fresh cilantro
1 teaspoon fresh ginger, thinly sliced
½ cup white grape or apple juice
Salt and pepper to taste
3 tablespoons finely-diced, tart apple for garnish

1. Thickly puree everything except the white grape juice, apple garnish, salt and pepper in small batches in a food processor. If the blade gets clogged add a little of the grape juice. The goal is to create a chunky liquid that preserves some of the texture.

2. Transfer the mix to a bowl and add any remaining grape juice. Stir and taste to check the seasoning and the acidity. Cover and chill 4 hours.

3. Ladle the soup into chilled bowls or mugs, and garnish with the diced apples.

FRESH CHILI CHICKEN CHILI

Each of the many times I have prepared this recipe I am skeptical that the recipe will work. Each and every time I have savored the results with pleasure. This is not a conventional approach to chili because it braises the chicken in the ground vegetables with delectable results. In the world of chilies not all have a piquant bite. The poblano chili and, less so, the Anaheim manage to have fresh pepper flavor with minimal heat. I prefer chicken thigh meat because the chili can simmer for a longer time without becoming overcooked and tough. Don't forget the garnishes; they are half the fun of a delicious bowl of chili. **Yields 6 to 8 servings.**

3 pounds boned and skinned raw chicken
    thighs, trimmed of excess fat, cut into
    bite size pieces
Salt and pepper to season chicken
1 tablespoon vegetable oil
One 4-ounce can roasted green chilies
4 poblano chilies, stemmed, seeded,
    and cut into large pieces
1 Anaheim chili pepper, stemmed, seeded,
    and cut into large pieces
2 medium onions, cut into large pieces (2 cups)
6 medium cloves garlic, minced
    (about 1 tablespoon)
4 teaspoons ground cumin
2 teaspoons ground coriander
1 teaspoon oregano
¾ teaspoon of salt
Two 15.5-ounce cans cannellini beans,
    drained and rinsed
3 cups low-sodium chicken broth
1 cup frozen corn
3 tablespoons fresh lime juice
    (from 2 to 3 limes)
¼ cup minced fresh cilantro leaves
4 scallions, white and light green parts
    sliced thin

1. In a blender, process the fresh and the canned chilies, onion, and garlic using short pulses until they become the consistency of chunky salsa. Add a little water or chicken stock to the blender if the vegetables won't circulate. Don't clean the blender yet!

2. Dry the chicken pieces with a paper towel and then season chicken with salt and pepper. Heat oil in large Dutch oven over medium-high heat until it just begins to smoke. Add half of the chicken and cook without moving until it is golden brown, about 3 minutes. Using tongs, turn chicken and lightly brown on opposite side, about 2 minutes. Transfer chicken to plate. Repeat with remaining chicken.

3. Pour off all but 1 tablespoon fat from the Dutch oven. Add the contents of the blender, cumin, coriander, oregano, and salt. Cover and simmer, stirring occasionally for about 10 minutes. Add all of the rinsed beans and simmer 5 more minutes.

4. To thicken the chili's consistency, puree two to four cups of the chili in the blender. Return the portion back to the pot and add the chicken stock. Add the seared chicken pieces and the corn. Reduce heat to medium-low and simmer for a final 12 minutes, covered, stirring occasionally.

5. With the heat off, add the lime juice, cilantro and scallions. Adjust seasonings with salt and pepper and serve.

6. Liven up the chili by serving it accompanied with grated cheese, non-fat sour cream, tortilla chips, and lime wedges.

Chicken Soup, Vietnamese-Style

A whiff of Asian fish sauce gives no clue of the magic it can work on a soup. As a background flavor with star anise and soy sauce it provides a deep, aromatic, and fulfilling flavor to this soup. On cool days our guests often are back for seconds of this soup. Serving the soup with a selection of vegetable toppings is fun for the guests and brings texture and unexpected flavor possibilities to the soup.
Yields 4 servings.

The Broth

5 cups low sodium chicken broth
3 tablespoons Asian fish sauce
1 tablespoon quality soy sauce
2 teaspoons granulated sugar
4 cloves garlic, peeled and crushed
2-inch piece fresh ginger, peeled, cut into
   dime-size rounds
2 star anise pods

Soup Garnish

1 whole 4-5 pound raw chicken, cut into sections
   (giblets removed); to save time, you could substitute
   a cooked supermarket rotisserie chicken
8 ounces dried flat rice noodles
4 cups Napa cabbage, rinsed and shredded
   thinly crosswise
2 scallions, white and green parts, sliced thinly
   on an angle
½ cup loose-packed fresh mint leaves, shredded
½ cup loose-packed fresh cilantro leaves, shredded
2 tablespoons chopped unsalted roasted peanuts

Other possible garnishes: shredded carrots, julienned snow peas, shredded zucchini, bean sprouts; 1 lime, cut into wedges

1. FOR THE BROTH: Bring the broth ingredients to a gentle boil in small stock pot over medium-high heat. Reduce heat to low; simmer partially covered for 10 minutes to blend flavors. Add the raw chicken to the broth and simmer until cooked through, about 15 minutes.

2. Remove chicken with slotted spoon and set aside. When cool enough to handle, strip off the skin and discard. Pull the meat from the bones and shred by hand into bite size pieces. Set aside the meat and discard the bones.

3. In a separate pot bring 4 quarts water to boil. Turn off the heat, break the noodles into thirds add to the hot water, and let sit until noodles are tender, 10 to 15 minutes. Drain.

4. Just before serving the soup, strain the star anise and ginger from the broth, then add the shredded cabbage, the chicken, and the scallions.

5. Serve immediately and pass small bowls of garnishes at the table.

POTATO-LEEK SOUP GOES GREEN

I offer a new take on the subtleties of potato leek soup that is sure to catch the eye with its luminescent color and vibrant flavors. We could also call this potato-leek-spinach-basil-toasted almond soup, but brevity has its place. Blanching the green leaves in a separate pot and puréeing them separately helps preserve the flavor and color of the soup. The toasted almonds in this recipe are blended into the soup with some reserved for a final crunchy soup garnish. This soup is more involved than others but the results are sublime. The potato leek portion of this soup can be made up to 3 days ahead of time, but add the green herb purée at the last minute because it darkens with reheating.

Yields 6 to 8 servings

4 medium leeks, white and light-green parts
   halved lengthwise, washed, and sliced thin
   (about 4 cups), reserve the green leek tops
3 cups low-sodium chicken broth
2 cups water
4 tablespoons (½ stick) unsalted butter
1 medium onion, chopped medium
   (about 1 cup)
1 teaspoon table salt
1 small russet potato (about 6 ounces),
   peeled, halved lengthwise,
   and cut into ¼-inch slices
1 bay leaf
1 (4-inch) sprig fresh thyme or tarragon
1 pound spinach washed and stemmed
2 cups basil leaves
1 tablespoon salt for the blanching water
¾ cup sliced almonds, toasted
   (reserve ¼ cup for garnish)
1 large slice sandwich bread dried
   or lightly toasted and torn up
Ground black pepper, salt

1. Prepare the leeks by removing the root ends and separating the green tops from the white base. The greens are too tough to eat but make a great stock by washing them and then boiling them for about a half hour in 2 cups of water and 3 cups of chicken stock. Cut the leek whites in half lengthwise and slice into ¼-inch thick half moons. Wash thoroughly and drain.

2. On low to medium heat, sauté the leek whites, onion, and salt with the butter. Reduce heat to low and cook, stirring frequently, until vegetables are softened, about 10 minutes.

3. Increase heat to high, stir in the chicken/leek broth, potato, bay leaf, and herb sprig and bring to boil. Reduce heat to low and simmer.

4. While the soup simmers, bring a separate pot with about 2 quarts of water to boil. Add 1 tablespoon of salt to this water. Plunge the spinach and basil leaves into this water until just wilted (about 30 seconds). Quickly drain the pot and submerge the leaves in cold water to stop the cooking process. Squeeze excess water out of the greens. A quick chop of the bunched greens will ease the blending process. Purée the blanched green leaves in a blender with a little of the soup stock. Set the green puree aside until the soup is ready to serve.

5. Toast the sliced almonds by pouring them onto a cookie tin and baking at 325 degrees until they begin to color and become fragrant (about 6-10 minutes).

6. By now the potatoes in the soup pot should be tender. Add the toasted bread and simmer until bread is completely saturated and starts to break down, about 5 minutes.

7. Remove and discard the bay leaf and herb sprig. Puréeing hot soup in a blender can be dangerous, so don't fill the blender more than two-thirds full. Add ½ cup of the toasted almonds to the blender, reserving the rest for garnish. Transfer the soup in batches to a blender and process until smooth and creamy. Transfer to large bowl and repeat with remaining soup.

8. Return soup to the saucepan and bring to a simmer; season with salt and pepper to taste. Add the spinach/basil mixture just before serving. Serve with remaining toasted almonds to garnish.

CHEDDAR, PEAR & HAM SANDWICH

We change the billing on the old standard ham and cheese marquis by allowing the aged cheddar to become the star, perked up with poached pear while letting the supporting credits go to the smoked ham. To speed up the pear poaching, the pears are sliced before poaching. The bread we prefer is a new, commonly available product (sometimes called Deli Thins) that resembles whole wheat English muffins but are much thinner and lower in calories. Focaccia bread or cranberry nut bread would also be delicious. Finally, to make this sandwich even grander, you have the option of adding spiced walnuts. It's a delicious combination first dreamed up by Tom Colicchio and Sisha Ortuzar in their collection called 'wichcraft.

Yields 4 sandwiches.

Poaching the Pears

⅔ cup sugar
⅔ cup cider vinegar
1 cup water
2 pieces star anise
1 teaspoon black peppercorns
2 whole cloves
Pinch of red pepper flakes
1 cinnamon stick
2 Bartlett pears, peeled, cored, and cut into
⅛-inch slices

The Sandwich Filling

8 slices sharp Cheddar cheese
8 slices smoked ham
4 whole wheat "Deli Thins"
Freshly ground black pepper
¼ cup spiced walnuts, if using
2 teaspoons stone-ground mustard

Optional spiced walnuts

¼ teaspoon ground cumin
¼ teaspoon ground cinnamon
¼ teaspoon grated nutmeg
1 tablespoon honey
1 cup walnut halves
½ teaspoon kosher salt

1. In a saucepan, combine the sugar, vinegar, water, star anise, peppercorns, cloves, red pepper flakes, and cinnamon stick and bring to a boil. Reduce the heat and simmer for 15 minutes.

2. Add the pears, bring back to a simmer, and cook for 2 to 3 minutes, until tender. Drain the pears and reserve the liquid for future use. If you are poaching these in advance, store the pears in the poaching liquid (these will keep in the refrigerator for 1 to 2 weeks).

3. Place 1 slice of cheese on each of 4 slices of bread. Top with the ham, followed by 4 to 6 slices of pear, and the walnuts, if using. Season with pepper and top with the remaining cheese. Spread the mustard on the remaining slices of bread.

4. Close the sandwiches. Warm a sauté pan to medium heat, add some of the butter. When the butter is melted, brown the sandwiches as you would a grilled cheese sandwich. This also works well in a sandwich press. Once cooked, remove, cut into halves, and serve.

Spiced walnuts

1. Preheat the oven to 300 degrees.

2. In a bowl, combine the cumin, cinnamon, and nutmeg and mix in the honey. Add the walnuts and toss to coat. Sprinkle with the salt.

3. Pour the nuts onto a greased sheet pan and toast in the oven. After six minutes stir the nuts and continue to bake about another 5 minutes, or until they are dark golden in color. Allow to cool completely before using or storing.

PISSALADIÈRE: A FRENCH PIZZA

This is so different from American pizza that it really is in a class by itself. Its popularity might take off in the states if it were just a little easier to pronounce! The sweetness of the caramelized onions and the saltiness of the anchovies make this French pizza outstanding. I'm taking a less traditional approach to this recipe by including Jim Lahey's no-knead pizza dough. Alternately, buy your raw dough already prepared from a grocery store or pizza shop. You can also save time by slicing the onions using a food processor. If you are not an anchovy fan, experiment with small amounts of an intensely flavored cheese. Toppings such as fresh herbs, peppers, or mushrooms will enhance the appearance of this pizza.

Serves 6 as a side dish.

The Crust
1½ cups + 2 tablespoons bread flour
1¼ teaspoons instant or active dry yeast
⅓ teaspoon salt
½ teaspoon sugar
½ cup + 3 tablespoons water, room temperature
Extra virgin olive oil for the pan

The Filling
3 tablespoons olive oil
2½ pounds onions, thinly sliced (about 8 cups)
3 garlic cloves, finely chopped
1 small bay leaf
1 teaspoon chopped fresh thyme
1 tablespoon drained capers
20 pitted Kalamata or Niçoise olives
16 anchovy fillets or blue cheese, parmesan,
    or good quality feta cheese

1. In a bowl, stir together the flour, yeast, salt, and sugar.

2. Add the water, and using a spoon, your hand, or a baker's plastic bench scraper, mix together until blended — about a minute. You will have a stiff dough once all of the flour is incorporated. The dough and filling can be prepared 1 day ahead if chilled. Let dough soften slightly at room temperature before rolling out.

3. Cover the dough and let rise at room temperature for about 2 hours. If your room is cold, put it in the oven with a pilot light to warm it up. If using a premade dough, let it come to room temperature.

4. Start your filling: Heat oil in heavy, large skillet over medium-low heat. Add onions, garlic, bay leaf, and thyme; stir to blend. Cover and cook until onions are very tender, stirring occasionally, about 12-20 minutes. Uncover and sauté until most liquid of the liquid evaporates and the onions start to brown. Stir frequently. Loosen the caramelized onions with a little water if necessary; these bits have the best flavor. The finished onions should be the color of light maple syrup, which takes about 10 more minutes.

5. Stir in capers. Season mixture with salt and pepper and discard the bay leaf. Cool to room temperature.

6. Preheat oven to 450 degrees. Set baking rack in top third of the oven.

7. Dump out the dough on a lightly-floured surface. Oil a 13x18 inch rimmed baking sheet liberally with extra virgin olive oil, then gently plop the dough on the pan and stretch and press it out to the edges. If it springs back (that's the gluten working), wait five minutes and then proceed. The thin dough may tear, but it's easy to patch it back together.

8. Spread cooked onion mixture evenly on top of the dough. Top decoratively with the olives, the anchovies and any other toppings you like. Bake until golden brown, about 10-15 minutes.

Spinach Pie with Feta and Dill

One of the few dishes that can be served at any time of day, this pie is portable, snackable, and nutritious. Traditionally baked inside layers of filo dough, the prep time has been shortened by using frozen spinach and a pre-baked crust. It is possible to reduce the fat even more by eliminating the pie crust and baking the filling in a greased pan sprinkled with cornmeal. While there are many versions of this ersatz quiche, I amended this Molly Katzen creation and it has become a dependable vegetarian entrée when the crowds arrive at Adelynrood. This pairs well with Tuscan Potato Salad and Luscious Lentil Soup. **Yields 8 portions.**

One 9-inch premade pie crust, uncooked
1 tablespoon olive oil
1½ cup finely diced onion
1 teaspoon minced fresh garlic
12 ounces frozen spinach, thawed,
　or two 8-ounce bags of fresh spinach,
　washed and stemmed
5 large eggs, beaten
1 cup ricotta cheese
1½ cups crumbled feta cheese
　(about 6 ounces by weight)
2 teaspoons fresh dill, chopped fine
Zest of one lemon plus 2 teaspoons
　lemon juice
½ teaspoon dried oregano
½ teaspoon ground nutmeg
¼ teaspoon black pepper
½ teaspoon salt

1. Thaw pie crust if frozen and preheat oven to 350 degrees. There is no need to pre-cook the pie crust.

2. If using fresh spinach, place it in a covered bowl and cook it on high in a microwave oven for about 45 seconds, or until just wilted. Whether fresh or frozen, the spinach needs to be squeezed out to remove as much water as possible. Chop spinach well.

3. Add the olive oil to a medium-hot pan. Sauté onions until soft, add the garlic and cook one minute more. Remove from heat.

4. Mix together the cooked onions, garlic, and all of the remaining ingredients. Take care to break up clumps of spinach. Taste the filling; depending on the type of feta cheese, you may need to add salt. Pour filling into pie crust.

5. Bake on the middle rack of the oven until the pie begins to puff up and the center of the pie has set, approximately 1 hour. After cooling, cut pie into 8 pieces. Serve warm. Stores up to 3 days in the refrigerator. Do not freeze.

TURKEY MUSHROOM BURGER

Here is a burger that is more savory than meaty. It is every bit as delicious as the beefy variety. We have given this understated meat some character so that it won't be lost amongst the condiments in the bun. Make mine a double!
Yields 6 patties.

¼ cup bread crumbs
3 tablespoons milk
2 eggs
1 pound raw, ground 85% lean turkey
1 cup raw, thinly sliced domestic mushrooms
2 tablespoons onions, finely chopped
2 tablespoons celery, finely chopped
2 tablespoons soy sauce
1 teaspoon Dijon mustard
1 teaspoon dried thyme
½ teaspoon salt
¼ teaspoon pepper
Buns and fixings

1. Soak the breadcrumbs in the milk for 10 minutes.

2. Whip the eggs until light and fluffy.

3. Combine all ingredients in a mixing bowl or a stand-up mixer. Note: the mushrooms do not need to be precooked.

4. The final mixture will be very wet and mushy. Scoop the burger mix directly into a hot, greased sauté pan. Unlike beef burgers, these burgers have very little shrinkage.

5. You may cook the burgers completely in the frying pan or you may finish the seared patties in a 350 degree oven until the interior reaches 165 degrees.

6. Garnish with tomatoes and lettuce. Warm the buns for extra credit. Got sliced cheese to serve on the side?

OUR
EVENING MEAL

POULTRY

Chicken Baja Dilla 58

Cornmeal Crunch Chicken
*   with Salsa Verde 60*

Moroccan Chicken and Vegetable Stew 62

Summer Chicken Stew
*   with Sweet Corn, Tomatoes, & Kale 64*

Rosemary Orange Chicken 66

Scallion Meatballs
*   with Pineapple-Ginger Glaze 68*

SEAFOOD

Charmoula the Great 69

Escabeche Style Trout
*   with Tomato Eggplant Relish 70*

RED MEAT

Cider-Brined Pork Chops 71

Ginger-Glazed Pork
*   with Middle Eastern Spice Rub 72*

Our Mini Meatloaves 73

Seekh Kebab 74

Spring Lamb Stew with Dill 75

Chicken Baja Dilla

With flavors redolent of southern Spain, this is a different take on the much loved, yet unexpected, medley inspired by The Silver Palate Cookbook. It works well with company because most of the preparation is completed the day before. Even better, whether served hot or at room temperature, the taste is just as delicious. I've chosen to use boneless thighs, but you could also substitute segmented whole chicken or even jointed chicken wings.
Two recommendations: *don't skip the overnight marinade, and skinning the chicken reduces the fat and makes the dish look better when served.*
Yields 6 to 8 servings.

3 pounds of boneless, skinless chicken thighs
2 teaspoons fresh garlic, chopped finely
2 tablespoons dried oregano
½ teaspoon salt
½ teaspoon black pepper
¼ cup red wine vinegar
¼ cup olive oil
½ cup pitted prunes, cut into quarters
½ cup dried apricots, cut into quarters
½ cup pitted Spanish green olives, sliced
½ cup capers with 2 tablespoons of caper juice
1 teaspoon Dijon mustard
4 bay leaves

Added just before roasting:
¼ cup brown sugar
1 cup white wine
1 large red bell pepper, seeded,
   cut into 1" long matchsticks

Garnish Added After Roasting
¼ cup toasted slivered almonds
¼ cup Italian parsley or cilantro, finely chopped

1. Trim any large pieces of fat from the thighs. Cut each thigh into 2 to 4 thumb-size pieces.

2. In a large bowl combine the chicken, garlic, oregano, salt, black pepper, vinegar, olive oil, prunes, apricots, olives, capers with caper juice, mustard, and bay leaves. Cover and let marinate in refrigerator overnight.

3. Preheat oven to 350 degrees. Arrange the chicken mixture with all of the marinade and the red peppers in a single layer in one or two large, shallow baking pans. Sprinkle chicken pieces with brown sugar and pour white wine around the borders of the pan.

4. Bake for 30-40 minutes. Chicken is done when the internal temperature of the meat reaches 165 degrees. Transfer to a serving platter. Sprinkle generously with parsley or cilantro and the slivered almonds. Pass remaining pan juices in a sauceboat.

Cornmeal Crunch Chicken
with Salsa Verde

If you thought those green, golf-ball-size fruits with the papery husks were green tomatoes, you were close. Tomatillos ("toma-tea-yos"), while in the same family as tomatoes, are closely related to the cape gooseberry. Fresh tomatillos have a tart flavor that mellows with heating. The combination of the tangy green sauce with the crispy yellow-crusted chicken is a treat for the mouth as well as the eyes. The sauce can be prepared up to two days ahead of time. Tomatillos naturally have lots of pectin, so don't be surprised if your sauce takes on a jelly-like texture when chilled.

Yields 4 servings

The Salsa

2 teaspoons canola oil
½ cup thinly sliced onion
2 cloves garlic, peeled and diced
½ teaspoon ground coriander
7 tomatillos, husked and rinsed and cut into
  quarters (canned tomatillos may be substituted)
4 tablespoons pumpkin seeds, divided
3 tablespoons chopped fresh cilantro, divided
1 cup chicken broth
½ teaspoon salt
¼ teaspoon ground pepper
½ lime, juiced (optional)

Crusted Chicken

4 boneless, skinless chicken breasts
  (1-1 ¼ pounds), trimmed
1 large egg white
2 tablespoons water
½ cup yellow cornmeal
¼ teaspoon each ground pepper and salt
¾ teaspoon ground cumin
3 teaspoons canola oil, divided

1. PREPARE THE SALSA: Add oil and then the onions to a warmed medium-sized saucepan. Sauté the onions for 3 to 4 minutes until translucent, then add the garlic and the coriander. Sauté for one minute more, then add the cut tomatillos. Reduce heat and sauté for 5 more minutes. Stir in the chicken broth.

2. Puree the contents of the pan in a blender with the cilantro, half the pumpkin seeds, salt, and pepper. Return the sauce to the pot for later warming.

3. THE CHICKEN: If the chicken breasts are large (more than 5 ounces each) flattening the chicken to an even consistency will help the cooking. To do this, place one piece of chicken at a time between sheets of plastic wrap and pound with a meat mallet or heavy skillet until flattened to an even ¼-inch thickness. Cut the flattened meat into desired portion sizes.

4. Mix egg white and water in a shallow dish until combined. Whisk cornmeal with the salt, pepper, and cumin in a shallow dish. Dip each chicken breast in egg white, then dredge in cornmeal mixture, turning to coat evenly. Heat 1½ teaspoons oil in a large nonstick skillet over medium heat. Cook 2 pieces of the chicken until the yellow corn meal crust starts to brown on the outside and the fillet is firm to the touch, 2 to 4 minutes per side. Transfer to a plate and tent with foil to keep warm. Wipe out the pan, reduce the heat slightly, and repeat with the remaining oil and chicken.

5. Warm the tomatillo sauce and taste to check the salt and pepper. If the sauce is not mildly tart, add the juice of half a lime to pucker it up a bit. Serve the chicken sitting in the sauce and garnished with the remaining 2 tablespoons of pumpkin seeds and 1 tablespoon cilantro.

Moroccan Chicken & Vegetable Stew

Sometimes I like to break up the pattern of traditional meals with a menu that has an exotic feel. I have seen plenty of skeptical guests, both the young and the graying, return for seconds of this delicious tagine. It is comfort food with an eastern accent whose many ingredients might look a little daunting but, in fact, there is nothing complicated about it. Because it reheats well, this dish can be prepared a day ahead. This westernized version of a tagine from The New Basics Cookbook *has been modified and enhanced.*

Yields 6 portions.

2 pounds boneless, skinless chicken thigh meat
2 tablespoons vegetable oil such as corn or canola
1½ cup onion, diced sugar cube size
3 cloves garlic, finely diced
2 cinnamon sticks
1 teaspoon curry powder
¾ teaspoon ground cumin
¼ teaspoon ground turmeric
¼ teaspoon pepper
½ teaspoon salt
4 cups chicken stock
1 cup carrots, peeled and sliced to a thick
    half moon shape
1 cup white (purple top) turnip, peeled and
    cut to sugar cube size
l large red bell pepper, cut into ¼ inch dice
3 ripe plum tomatoes, seeded and cut
    into ½ inch dice
1 cup pitted prunes, quartered
¼ cup dried currants
1 cup chick peas, drained and rinsed
1½ cup zucchini, cut to sugar cube size
1 tablespoon cornstarch
1 tablespoon chopped cilantro or parsley

1. Pat the chicken thighs dry to improve their browning. Cut the thighs into bite size pieces, usually that will be in quarters.

2. Heat oil in a large Dutch oven until it begins to smoke. It is better to sear the chicken in small batches than it is to overcrowd the pan. Brown the thighs on both sides, but don't cook the chicken all the way through. Using a slotted spoon, transfer the chicken to a dish and set aside.

3. Sauté the onions on medium-low heat in the same Dutch oven, adding additional oil if needed. After four minutes, add the garlic to the Dutch oven and cook over low heat for two minutes. Stir in the dry spices: cinnamon sticks, curry powder, cumin, turmeric, pepper and salt. Add the chicken stock and bring the liquid to a boil. Reduce the heat to a simmer and continue cooking for 5 minutes.

4. Add the seared chicken thighs, carrots, turnip and bell pepper. Simmer for 10 minutes. Add the tomatoes, prunes, currants and chick peas. Simmer an additional 10 minutes. Taste the stew to check the seasoning.

5. Remove the cinnamon sticks and discard. Add the zucchini to the pot. Mix the cornstarch with a tablespoon of cold water to make a slurry. Add this slurry to the pot while stirring. When it starts to boil again, remove from heat. Transfer to serving bowls and garnish with chopped cilantro or parsley. This dish is wonderful served with couscous or rice.

SUMMER CHICKEN STEW
WITH SWEET CORN, TOMATOES & KALE

It makes sense that certain comfort foods are shared by cultures throughout the world. These kin of the culinary family: the stew, ragout, fricassee, tagine, eintopf, zharkoye, to name a few, braise together meat and vegetables to create tender savory meal-in-a-pot entrees. I offer two variations but you do not have to think hard to adapt seasonal foods to the basic premise of searing the meat and then slow cooking it with flavorful broth and vegetables. The summer stew changes to autumn stew by removing the corn, lime, and okra and adding red wine, mushrooms, baby onions, parsnips, and rosemary. Rice, roasted root vegetables, or couscous pair well with chicken stews but will never outshine fluffy mashed potatoes.

Yields 6 Servings.

Carolina Wren

4 ears of fresh sweet corn (3 cups kernels)
6 cups chopped kale, coarse stems removed
3 tablespoons vegetable oil
2 pounds boneless, skinless chicken thighs
2 medium leeks (white parts only) or
    2 medium onions, cut into ½-inch
    dice-sized pieces
3 cups chicken broth
¾ teaspoon salt
½ teaspoon pepper
1 tablespoon cornstarch
one 12-ounce can of cannellini beans
    or black-eyed peas, rinsed
2 plum tomatoes, seeded and cut into
    ½-inch dice-sized pieces
1 cup chopped okra
3 tablespoons coarsely chopped cilantro
1 teaspoon grated lime zest
¼ cup fresh lime juice

1. Remove the corn kernels from the cobs. Scrape the cobs with the back of the knife to extract the "cream" from the corn. Set aside kernels and corn cream.

2. Steam or blanch the chopped kale in several quarts of boiling salted water for 5 minutes or until just tender. Immerse the kale in cold water to stop the cooking process, then drain and set aside.

3. Cut the chicken into medium bite size pieces, about 1 inch square. Dry the pieces with a towel and sprinkle lightly with salt. Heat vegetable oil in thick-bottomed Dutch oven until the oil just begins to smoke. Carefully add just enough chicken to fill a single layer. A grease screen or a loose lid will help control the splatter. Turn the chicken when the exterior has browned. After two more minutes, remove the chicken to a plate and continue with the next batch. By the end, the pan will become lightly encrusted. This browning provides a superb flavor base for the stew, so don't wash it out!

4. Using the same pan at medium-low heat (add a little olive oil if necessary) add the leeks or onions. Simmer about 5 minutes until soft. Add chicken broth and scrape the bottom of the pot to loosen the flavorful bits. Bring to simmer.

5. Add the seared chicken and the salt and pepper to the chicken stock and simmer for 15 minutes.

6. Mix the cornstarch with 1 tablespoon of cold water and stir to make a slurry. While stirring, gradually add the slurry to the simmering broth.

7. Add the corn, beans, tomatoes, and okra to the pot. Simmer for 5 minutes.

8. With the heat off, add the steamed kale, cilantro, lime zest, and lime juice to the pot. Taste to check the seasoning. Serve piping hot.

Rosemary & Orange Braised Chicken

Tender chicken almost falling off the bone, infused with the unexpected combination of herbs and fruit. Not sure which feeds the anticipation of this home-style comfort food more: the tantalizing aroma or the vibrant colors of the chicken and vegetables. A crusty bread to soak up the sauce is a given, but rice or roasted potatoes also make a fine accompaniment.

Yields 4 to 5 portions.

4 tablespoons olive oil, divided

One 3-4 pound chicken cut at the joints into 8 pieces; discard the skin

Salt and freshly ground pepper to taste

1 cup of ½ inch diced yellow onion

1 cup carrots, peeled and chopped in ½ inch rounds

4 garlic cloves minced

1 cup chicken stock

½ cup orange juice

½ cup canned, crushed tomatoes

2 tablespoon fresh rosemary, stemmed and minced

1 red bell pepper, seeded and cut into julienne

1 cup zucchini, cut in half lengthwise and sliced ¼ inch thick at an angle

1 cup yellow summer squash cut same as zucchini

2 teaspoons arrowroot or cornstarch mixed with 2 teaspoons water

⅓ cup chopped parsley

grated zest of 1 orange

1. Heat 3 tablespoons of the oil to high heat in a heavy bottomed Dutch oven or skillet. Pat the chicken pieces dry and season them with salt and pepper. Carefully add the chicken pieces to the hot oil two or three at a time. Turn pieces over once the meat lightly browns (about 2 minutes), then remove chicken from the pan and set aside.

2. Reduce the heat to low/medium, and, using any leftover oil, add the onions to the skillet. When the onions have turned translucent add the carrots and garlic and cook gently another 5 minutes, stirring frequently.

3. Add the chicken stock, orange juice, tomatoes, and half of the rosemary. Scrape any browned bits from the bottom of the pan. Season to taste with salt and pepper and simmer the mixture, uncovered, for 15 minutes.

4. Return chicken pieces to the pan and simmer with a lid on top for 15 minutes. Turn the pieces over and simmer another 10 minutes or until fully cooked. If you wish, you may complete the recipe to this point the day before serving. You can refrigerate the chicken in the sauce and reheat gently before proceeding.

5. Mix the arrowroot with the water. While stirring the pot, gradually add this slurry to the hot liquid.

6. When the pot begins to simmer add the bell peppers, zucchini, yellow squash, orange zest, and the remaining rosemary. Season with salt and pepper. Turn off the heat and let sit with a cover for a few minutes.

7. Before serving, sprinkle with the chopped parsley.

SCALLION MEATBALLS WITH PINEAPPLE-GINGER GLAZE

What if spaghetti and meatballs went Asian? These full-flavored turkey meatballs are lighter on the fat but still spirited and juicy. (Isn't that how we all want to be?) They can be served on toothpicks as an appetizer or as an inventive main course atop buckwheat or egg noodles or even rice.
Yields about two dozen small meatballs or 12 larger size.

FOR THE MEATBALLS

1 pound ground turkey
4 large or 6 small scallions, finely chopped
6 ounces water chestnuts, diced in small bits
1 bunch cilantro, finely chopped (about 1 cup);
  reserve 1 tablespoon for garnish
2 tablespoons peeled fresh ginger grated or
  chopped finely
1 egg, lightly beaten
¼ cup bread crumbs, preferably Japanese panko crumbs
2 tablespoons sesame oil
2 tablespoons soy sauce
½ teaspoon freshly ground black pepper

THE SAUCE

1¾ cup pineapple juice
2 tablespoons white vinegar
¾ cup soy sauce
½ cup packed light brown sugar
1 tablespoon peeled fresh ginger, grated, or
  chopped finely
1 teaspoon chopped garlic
2 tablespoons cornstarch
2 tablespoons water
1 teaspoon sesame oil
2 teaspoons scallion whites, sliced finely for garnish

1. MAKE THE MEATBALLS: Preheat oven to 350 degrees.

2. Mix the turkey, scallions, water chestnuts, cilantro, ginger, egg, sesame oil, soy sauce, breadcrumbs, and pepper in a bowl. The balls will be sticky but should hold their shape. Add more breadcrumbs if the balls feel loose.

3. Roll mixture into golf-ball-size balls. Place the balls on a greased or non-stick sheet pan. Bake for 15 minutes at 350 degrees or until internal temperature reaches 160 degrees.

4. MAKE THE GINGER SAUCE: Stir together the pineapple juice, vinegar, soy sauce, brown sugar, ginger, and garlic in a medium saucepan. Bring to a boil and then lower the flame and simmer for 10 minutes.

5. Dissolve the cornstarch in water. While stirring the pot add the cornstarch slurry to the simmering sauce. Briefly bring the sauce back to a boil until it thickens. Remove from heat and add the sesame oil. Taste the sauce, checking for seasoning and tartness. Sauce and meatballs can be made up to 2 days ahead and refrigerated.

6. Let the sauce coat the meatballs and finish with chopped scallions and the reserved cilantro sprigs.

CHARMOULA THE GREAT

This is one of my favorite seafood preparations because it gives otherwise un-noteworthy seafood a wallop of interesting flavors with minimal fuss. Charmoula is a traditional North African marinade of herbs, spices and lemon that becomes a sauce as the fish cooks. In her book, The Healthy Hedonist, *Myra Kornfeld boosts the texture and presentation of the fish by baking it on top of a bed of sautéed Mediterranean vegetables. Overall, it's a striking and sophisticated combination that leaves you looking like a seasoned chef. This recipe adapts well to other seafood and meats.*
Yields 4 servings.

THE CHARMOULA SAUCE
¼ cup extra virgin olive oil
3 cloves minced garlic
¼ cup parsley leaves
¼ cup cilantro leaves
1 teaspoon paprika
1 teaspoon ground cumin
4 tablespoons fresh lemon juice
½ teaspoon salt
¼ teaspoon fresh ground black pepper

THE VEGETABLE BASE
1 tablespoon extra virgin olive oil
1 cup red onion, thinly sliced
½ teaspoon ground coriander
Pinch of cayenne or red pepper flakes
¼ cup sun-dried tomatoes, soaked in warm water until softened, drained and cut into thin strips
1 bulb of fennel, sliced thinly. Save some of the green fronds for garnish.
½ cup pitted Gaeta or Kalamata olives, cut in half and rinsed

Four 5-ounce pieces of striped bass, red snapper or most any thick white fish skinned fillets.

1. Preheat the oven to 400 degrees. Have ready a shallow casserole dish for baking the fish.

2. In a blender or food processor, blend the olive oil, chopped garlic, parsley, cilantro, paprika, cumin, lemon juice, salt, and pepper. Reserve half of this mixture to top the fish when it comes out of the oven. Coat the fish with the rest of the charmoula and refrigerate.

3. Warm 1 tablespoon of the olive oil in a medium skillet. Sauté the onions until softened over medium-low heat, about 10 minutes. Add the coriander, the cayenne, the sun-dried tomatoes, the fennel, and the olives. Sauté on low for two minutes. Line the bottom of the casserole dish with this onion mixture.

4. Place the fish on top of the onion mixture. Bake from 10 to 20 minutes (depending on the thickness of the fish) or until the fish is cooked through and opaque. If you are uncertain about doneness, you can examine the texture of the fish by making a tiny slit in the thickest part of the fish.

5. As soon as the fish comes out of the oven, brush the remaining charmoula on top of the fish. Garnish with the chopped fennel fronds. Serve hot with good bread to soak up the fragrant sauce.

ESCABECHE-STYLE TROUT WITH TOMATO RELISH

Most of us are used to marinating a meat before cooking it, but this delicious recipe develops its character by letting the cooked fish soak up the flavors of a simple homemade relish before serving. Escabeche is often served in the warmer months in countries from Persia to Spain, either cold or at room temperature. Allow the cooked fish at least an hour to sit with the eggplant relish so it can absorb the flavors. This dish gets even better when accompanied by a rice salad or roasted potatoes. Extra eggplant relish stores well in the refrigerator and makes a nice addition to salads or on top of toasted bread. **Yields 4 servings.**

THE RELISH

**1 medium eggplant, peeled and
   cut to sugar cube size**
1 cup diced Spanish onion
1 tablespoon salt
2 tablespoons olive oil
7 cloves of garlic, finely diced
1 teaspoon sage
1 teaspoon thyme
1 teaspoon ground black pepper
1 pint grape tomatoes, cut into quarters
½ cup apple cider vinegar
3 tablespoons honey

THE FISH

**Four 4-ounce portions of filleted trout
   (skin on)**
¼ cup all-purpose flour
½ teaspoon salt
¼ teaspoon ground black pepper
¼ teaspoon cumin
2 tablespoons olive oil
1 avocado sliced for garnish

1. Toss the eggplant and salt together and let sit in a colander for at least 1 hour. This will draw out any bitterness and improve the finished texture. Rinse the eggplant and squeeze the cubes tightly to remove any excess water.

2. Warm the olive oil in a large sauté pan over medium heat. Add the onions and cook for 2 minutes. Stir in the garlic and gently cook for another minute before adding the eggplant and the dried herbs. A slow simmer will yield the best texture. If you use fresh herbs, add them at the end of the cooking process. Stir the mixture occasionally and continue to cook until the eggplant softens, about 8 minutes.

3. Meanwhile heat the honey and vinegar together in a microwave or separate pot.

4. Remove the eggplant mixture from the heat. Add the quartered tomatoes and the vinegar mixture. Transfer the relish to a bowl and rinse the pan in order to sauté the fish.

5. On a pie plate, mix together the flour, cumin, salt, and pepper. Heat the sauté pan to medium/high heat and add the olive oil. Dredge the fish in the flour mixture, being careful to shake off excess flour. Sauté the fish approximately 3 minutes on each side or until lightly browned.

6. Lay the cooked fish on a casserole dish. Top with the eggplant tomato relish and some of its sauce. Just before serving garnish with the avocado slices.

Cider-Brined Pork Chops

Brining is a simple way to infuse flavor and moisture into relatively lean meats. Soaking raw meat in a brining solution draws in flavor and reduces the toughness of the meats. I have heard overwhelmingly positive responses from our diners when serving brined meats. The brining solution in this recipe is somewhere between a marinade and a brine in that it lets the cider and herb flavors permeate the meat, while using less salt than a standard brine. It works best with thicker pork chops, but I have used it successfully with supermarket thin-cut chops. If you are using a coarser salt, like a kosher, remember that coarse salt weighs less by volume so you will need to increase the quantity by 50% to about ⅓ cup of salt. Salt substitutes that use potassium chloride also work well. These chops also taste delicious when grilled over moderate heat. **Yields 4 servings.**

4 center-cut pork loin chops,
   1¼ to 1½ inches thick
Olive oil for the sauté

Brining Solution
4 cups water
2 cups apple cider
¼ cup table salt
½ cup light brown sugar
10 whole peppercorns
4 bay leaves
½ bunch fresh thyme or
   2 teaspoons dried thyme
1 onion, chopped
1 carrot, peeled and chopped
1 celery rib, chopped

The Garnish
½ red onion, peeled and cut into
   ¼ inch thick half moons
2 Granny Smith apples, peeled, seeded and
   cut into sections as if for apple pie

1. To make the brine, combine all brine ingredients in a saucepan. Bring to a boil over high heat, then remove from heat and let cool.

2. Add the pork chops to the cooled brine. It is best if the chops are completely submerged. Sometimes a plate will help to weigh down the chops. Refrigerate for 12 to 24 hours.

3. Drain the brine mixture and discard the brine. Pat the meat dry with a towel. Add just enough oil to coat the bottom of the skillet. When the skillet is hot, add the chops and reduce heat to moderate. Cook for about 10 minutes for thicker chops, then turn and cook until the chops are no longer pink at the bone, about 10 minutes longer.

4. Set aside the chops on a plate. Increase the heat of the pan to medium hot. Add a little olive oil if necessary. Sauté the onions until they begin to soften, then remove from pan. Sauté the apples until they begin to soften. Serve the pork chops hot on a bed of the onions with the cooked apples on the side.

GINGER GLAZED PORK WITH MIDDLE EASTERN SPICE RUB

This recipe blends culinary traditions to create a succulent roast pork that has been a favorite here since its introduction. The spice rub lasts up to six months and can be used with almost any roasted or grilled meat. It is possible to use pre-ground spices but the flavors will not be the same. Save a little time with a bottled Asian plum sauce, ginger jam, or even an apricot spread with a little ginger added. Do be extra careful not to over cook the relatively small tenderloins, which go from moist and tender to dry and featureless in just a few minutes.

Yields 6 portions.

Two 1-pound pork tenderloins
   (do not trim)

SPICE RUB
1 tablespoon cumin seeds
1½ teaspoons coriander seeds
1 teaspoon fennel seeds
½ teaspoon ground cinnamon
¼ teaspoon ground allspice

SEARING AND GARNISHING
4 tablespoons vegetable oil
3 Granny Smith apples, peeled, seeded
   and cut to the size of orange sections
Bottled plum sauce or ginger jam
2 scallions sliced thinly, greens only

Helpful Hint: *It's a good practice to sniff your spices when you open the jar. Fresh spices should be remarkably aromatic, but as they sit in the cabinet the flavors dissipate to almost nothing over a year's time (some would say 6 months). Exceptions include whole seeds like cumin, coriander, or whole cloves. Bland spices do nothing but take up space.*

1. Preheat oven to 350 degrees.

2. Combine cumin, coriander, and fennel seeds in small skillet. Stirring frequently, toast the seeds over medium heat until fragrant, about 2 minutes, and then cool to room temperature; grind the spices with a mortar and pestle or spice mill. Transfer to a small bowl; stir in cinnamon and allspice.

3. Dry the raw pork tenderloin. Coat the meat with the spice mix. In a sauté pan warmed to medium heat, sear the pork in half of the oil, just until the crust begins to color. High heat will cause the coating to become bitter. Transfer the meat to a roasting pan and bake for approximately 10 to 15 minutes.

4. Wipe out the sauté pan and bring it to high heat. Add the rest of the oil. When the hot oil starts to shimmer, carefully add the apple slices. Let the slices sit so they lightly brown, about 1 to 2 minutes. Stir and repeat. The goal is to have slightly firm apples that still taste a little tart. When done, transfer the apples to a plate and cover.

5. When the pork reaches 125 degrees (as registered by inserting a meat thermometer into the thickest part of the meat) remove it from the oven and brush on the plum sauce. Return to the oven and cook until the internal temperature reaches 140 degrees.

6. Immediately give the meat a final brush with the plum sauce. Let the meat sit in a warm place for at least 20 minutes before slicing. Slice in ½ inch rounds and serve garnished with the warm apples and a scattering of scallions.

Our Mini Meatloaves

At Adelynrood when we've had enough of the exotic, the vegetarian, or the seasonal entrées, the meat and potatoes crowd has been known to give a cheer when good old meatloaf returns to the menu. My favorite part of this recipe variation, inspired by Cook's Country Magazine, is the glaze on top and how well it works with the beef. We serve our meatloaves as individual mini loaves, but there is no reason you couldn't roast them in a loaf pan as long as you increase the cooking time. This recipe can be mixed a day ahead and refrigerated if needed.

Yields 4 to 6 servings.

⅔ cup fine breadcrumbs
¼ cup milk
3 tablespoon Worcestershire sauce
¼ cup minced fresh parsley leaves
1½ tablespoon Dijon mustard
1 large egg
1 teaspoon onion powder
1 teaspoon garlic powder
⅛ teaspoon cayenne pepper
½ teaspoon each salt and pepper
1½ pound 85/15 ground beef
  (85% lean/15% fat)

The glaze
½ cup ketchup
¼ cup packed light brown sugar
4 teaspoons apple cider vinegar

1. THE MEATLOAVES: Preheat oven to 375 degrees. Set an oven rack on the top third of the oven.

2. Mix breadcrumbs, milk, Worcestershire, parsley, mustard, egg, onion powder, garlic powder, cayenne, salt, and pepper in a large bowl. Add meat and mix with hands until thoroughly combined. Form into 4 tightly-packed loaves, each measuring 4 by 3 inches. They may seem large but they will shrink considerably when cooking. Place the mini-loaves on a baking sheet or on a broiler pan to allow the fat to drain off when cooking.

3. Roast the meatloaves until they are ¾ cooked, about 20 minutes.

4. FOR THE GLAZE: While meat is browning, combine ketchup, brown sugar, and vinegar in bowl.

5. Remove the pan from the oven and increase the heat to 450 degrees. Brush the glaze on the loaves and return to oven for a final 5 minutes.

6. Bake until a thermometer inserted in the middle of the loaf registers 160 degrees. While the loaves rest on the cooking pan, brush once more with the glaze. Serve, passing the remaining glaze separately.

SEEKH KEBAB

There are hundreds of varieties of kebab; not all of them are cooked on a skewer, and many have assertive spices that make plain meat and vegetable kebobs seem boring. This list of ingredients may look long but these delicious ground meat patties from India come together easily. Wrapped in warm pita bread with lettuce, tomato and yogurt sauce on top, they are irresistible.

Yields 5 portions.

THE KEBABS
1 pound of lean ground beef or lamb
1 medium onion, finely minced
1 clove garlic, finely minced
1 teaspoon of ginger root, finely minced
1½ teaspoons of salt
1 teaspoon fresh ground pepper
2 teaspoons ground cumin
½ teaspoon ground coriander
¼ teaspoon ground cloves
teaspoon crushed dried red peppers
Juice of 1 lime
½ cup of plain, low-fat yogurt
2 tablespoons vegetable oil

THE YOGURT SAUCE
8 oz. plain cold yogurt, preferably Greek style
1 garlic clove, minced
1 tablespoon lemon juice
Salt to taste

SANDWICH TOPPINGS
5 pieces pita bread or naan bread
2 cups shredded lettuce
1 cup diced tomatoes

1. For the patties, combine all ingredients except those for the yogurt sauce and knead thoroughly with your hands. Chill for at least 2 hours.

2. Meanwhile, make the yogurt sauce. In a small mixing bowl, combine yogurt, lemon juice, garlic, and salt. Mix well.

3. Form lamb (or beef) mixture into 2-inch patties and cook over a grill set at medium heat. These can also be baked on a jelly roll pan in a preheated oven at 400 degrees for about 10 minutes or until internal temperature reaches 165 degrees.

4. Serve hot, wrapped in warm pita bread with shredded lettuce, diced tomatoes, and yogurt sauce drizzled on top. Alternately, serve on top of a bed of white rice cooked with a few lentils and garnish with caramelized onions.

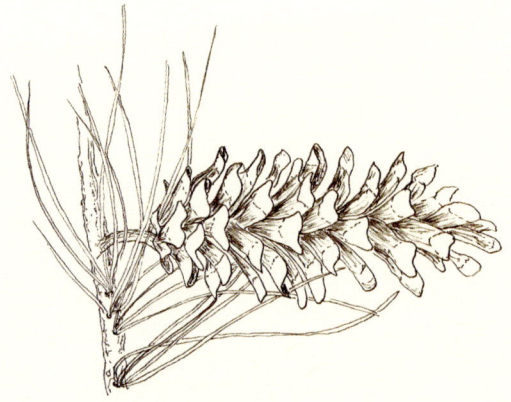

Spring Lamb Stew with Dill

I'm not the biggest fan of dill, but this classic Scandinavian blend of lemon, dill, and braised lamb changed my mind forever. It is mouth-wateringly scrumptious. Add the optional sour cream and serve it over noodles. If you want to save time, you can buy precut lamb stew meat. In any case, be sure the fat is well trimmed. Shelburne Farms of Vermont gets the credit for reviving this enduring dish.

Yields 4 to 6 portions.

1½ pounds lamb stew meat,
   cut into 1½ inch pieces
1½ teaspoons kosher salt (plus more to taste)
3-4 tablespoons vegetable oil
1-2 tablespoons of olive oil
1 medium onion halved and thinly sliced
1 cup dry white wine
2 tablespoons all-purpose flour
2 cups low-sodium chicken broth
2 cups carrots, peeled and cut into
   thick half moons
2 cups frozen peas, thawed
2 tablespoons chopped fresh dill,
   plus extra for garnish
1½ cups sour cream, optional
   (do not use non-fat sour cream)
1 teaspoon lemon zest
1-2 teaspoons fresh lemon juice
Freshly ground pepper to taste

1. Pat the lamb dry and sprinkle on the salt.

2. In a large sauté pan set over medium-high heat, heat 2 tablespoons of the vegetable oil. When the oil is very hot, brown the lamb, in batches, if necessary, so as not to crowd the pan, adding more oil as needed. Sear the meat until a nice golden brown crust develops on each side, 2-3 minutes per side. If you have excess oil in the pan, pour it off and discard, but don't wash the pan. Transfer the seared lamb to a plate.

3. Add the olive oil to the same pan, and then add the onion. Cook, stirring occasionally, for 2-3 minutes, until the onion has softened and colored. Stir in the flour, then add the white wine and deglaze the pan, stirring to scrape up any brown bits. Simmer for 2-3 minutes.

4. Add the chicken stock and the carrots and bring to a simmer. Add the lamb and any accumulated juices back to the pan. Cover the pot and maintain a gentle simmer for about 1 hour, or until the lamb is tender.

5. Stir in the peas, the chopped dill, lemon zest, 1 teaspoon of the lemon juice, the remaining ½ teaspoon of salt, and the sour cream (if using). Do not allow the mixture to boil. Let the covered pot sit without heat for 5 minutes.

6. Sample the sauce to see if it needs more salt or pepper. Serve garnished with additional fresh dill, if desired.

SUNDRY SAVORIES

Eggplant Stacks 78
Fresh Peach Salsa 79
Muhammara Dip 80
Stuffed Zucchini Boats 81

EGGPLANT STACKS

The delicacy of eggplant is often lost in American style eggplant parmesan with its coatings and profusions of goopy melted cheese. The simplicity of this recipe lets the roasted eggplant take a soliloquy to state its subtle case. The roasted eggplant rounds are served with a light tomato sauce and broiled cheese on top. We serve the stacks as a side dish, but by adding a little herbed ricotta between the layers the stacks become a tasteful center of the plate entree. Serve with a pasta or risotto on the side and, presto, you have the makings of a meal. **Yields 5 to 7 portions.**

THE EGGPLANT
2 large firm eggplants,
   cut into ½" rounds
2 tablespoons olive oil
Salt and pepper to taste
1 teaspoon oregano

THE TOMATO SAUCE
2 tablespoons olive oil
1 small onion, finely diced
2 garlic cloves, diced
One 28-ounce can of small
   diced tomatoes
½ teaspoon salt
1 teaspoon dried basil
Pinch of sugar, if needed

TO GARNISH THE EGGPLANT
2 tablespoons fresh basil
   or parsley, chopped
3 ripe plum tomatoes, sliced in
   ¼" thick rounds
¼ cup Asiago cheese, grated
   or sliced

1. Preheat oven to 400 degrees. Grease a large cookie tin. With a brush or your hands, rub the olive oil onto the eggplant slices. Lay out the eggplant on the cookie sheet and sprinkle with salt, pepper and the oregano.

2. Roast the eggplant on the top shelf of the oven for 15 minutes or until the tops have slightly browned and the center of the eggplant depresses easily.

3. THE SAUCE: While the eggplant roasts, heat a medium-size saucepan to medium heat. Add the olive oil and then the onions. When the onions turn translucent after 4 to 5 minutes, add the garlic and sauté for a minute more. Add the finely diced tomatoes with their juice and the salt. Stir in basil and turn the heat down to low. Simmer this sauce 10 minutes. Remove the pan from the heat and check the seasoning with a quick taste. If it tastes too acidic, add a pinch of sugar.

4. ASSEMBLE: Pour all but a ¼ cup of the sauce into an 11" x 7" baking pan. Lay out one layer of the cooked eggplant over the sauce. Place two slices of tomato on top of each eggplant slice. Top each one with a second layer of eggplant and a sprinkling of cheese. Up to this point this dish may be prepared and refrigerated one day ahead (when re-heating the chilled eggplant, warm it for 15 minutes in a 350 degree oven before proceeding to step 5).

5. Allow the broiler to warm up. Broil the eggplant just until cheese melts and begins to bubble. Remove from oven.

6. Garnish the tops of each eggplant stack with a dollop of the reserved tomato sauce and a sprinkling of fresh herbs. Serve warm.

FRESH PEACH SALSA

I adore this salsa with grilled meats or almost any fish. In fact, one of our kitchen staff preferred the salsa to the rest of the meal and wanted only peach salsa. This recipe can be adapted to other stone fruits such as nectarines, mangoes, or plums. The red onions will mellow as they sit in the fruit juices.

2 cups peeled, diced ripe peaches
   (about 2 medium-size peaches)
½ cup diced red onion
½ cup finely diced red pepper
½ to ¾ teaspoon finely minced jalapeno chili,
   with seeds and ribs removed
2 teaspoons olive oil
2 tablespoons lime juice
¼ cup minced fresh mint
2 teaspoons grated fresh ginger
¼ teaspoon salt

Combine all ingredients and let sit, unrefrigerated, for
at least 30 minutes to let the flavors mingle, then serve.

Muhammara Dip

So many of our guests can't quite figure out what the delectable flavors within this are. This versatile Syrian recipe can be a dip, a sandwich spread, a pasta sauce, or thinned to become a marinade for kebobs. Its flavor is fresh and distinctive. Toasted walnuts and roasted red peppers provide the body, while tomato and a splash of pomegranate molasses lend the dish a subtly sweet back note. My personal favorite is to enjoy it as a dip with pita chips. If you can't find the ever-useful pomegranate molasses in the ethnic foods aisle, a passable substitute can be made with equal parts honey and balsamic vinegar. For the roasted peppers you could use canned roasted peppers in a pinch, but the flavor will not be the same. Preparing Muhammara a day prior to serving will improve the flavors and, if stored in a sealed container, it will last up to 10 days in the refrigerator. **Yields about 2 cups.**

2 large red bell peppers, roasted, seeded, and peeled
¼ teaspoon ground cumin
⅓ cup walnuts, toasted
⅛ cup whole-grain bread crumbs
1 tablespoon pomegranate molasses
2 tablespoons tomato paste
Pinch crushed red pepper flakes or
     ½ seeded jalapeño chili
¼ to ½ cup warm water (depending on
     desired consistency)
½ teaspoon fine-grain sea salt
2 tablespoons extra-virgin olive oil

1. If you have a gas stove, the easiest way to roast the peppers is to lightly oil them, then place them directly on top of the burner. Rotate every minute or so as the skin blackens. Turn on your exhaust fan or your smoke detector might soon be blaring! If using a broiler or grill, cut the very top and bottom of the peppers off, remove the seeds and ribs, then make a single cut to open up the peppers so they can lay flat. Lightly oil the peppers so the high heat can blacken the skin side only.

2. Placing the blackened peppers in a covered bowl for 10 minutes will help separate the charred skin from the peppers. You can wipe the peppers but don't rinse them because you will lose the best part of the flavor. Discard stem and all pepper seeds.

3. Add the peppers and the remaining ingredients (except the olive oil) to a blender or food processor. Puree until smooth. Slowly drizzle in the olive oil while the motor is running.

4. Taste to correct the seasoning and acidity.

Stuffed Zucchini Boats

Ah, what to do with these gorgeous green squashes when the garden flourishes with just a little too much abundance? No more mushy, cut-up, sautéed vegetable medleys. Stuff the blanched zucchinis and brown them in the oven. This dairy and herb filling is but one of many possibilities for stuffing and provides a great opportunity to utilize leftovers: whole, cooked grains, like rice or barley, can be combined with leftover meats and vegetables.

Yields 6 to 8 portions

4 medium zucchinis, about 2 pounds total
¾ cup shredded sharp cheddar cheese
¼ cup small curd cottage cheese
1 large egg, beaten
3 tablespoons minced fresh parsley
1 teaspoon thinly sliced scallions
1 stalk celery, finely diced
¼ cup breadcrumbs
½ teaspoon dried oregano or thyme or dill
Salt and pepper to taste
Paprika (optional)

1. Preheat the oven to 350 degrees and lightly oil a baking sheet or casserole pan.

2. Bring a large saucepan of water to a gentle boil. Carefully add the uncut zucchinis to the water and simmer for 4 to 5 minutes. You'll know the zucchinis are ready when you poke them with a knife and the flesh is tender. It's better for them to be a little too firm than overcooked. Drain and cool the zucchinis.

3. This is one of few recipes where we don't cut the ends off the zucchini because they help hold the filling in. Divide each zucchini lengthwise. With a teaspoon, carve out and reserve the core of each zucchini, leaving a raised area on each end. If the zucchini is longer than your hand, leave a raised area at the halfway point to create two "canoes" from each half.

4. Finely chop the zucchini pulp and squeeze out any excess water.

5. In a medium bowl mix together the zucchini pulp, cheddar cheese, cottage cheese, egg, parsley, scallions, herbs, breadcrumbs, salt, and pepper.

6. Stuff the zucchini halves with the filling. Place the filled halves on the baking sheet with the filling side up. Bake for 10-15 minutes until filling has set. If you have a broiler, a final 2 to 3 minutes beneath the broiler will give you a delectable golden brown topping. If desired, dust lightly with paprika before serving.

Sensible Sweets & Lavish Indulgences

Almond Cake with Chamomile 84

Almond Stuffed Poached Pears 85

Chocolate Go Ahead Cookies 86

Deep Dark Chocolate Bundt Cake 88

Florentine Bars 89

Full of Fruit Bars 90

Ginger Dreams 91

Heavenly Honey Seared Pineapple 92

Indian Pudding Cake 93

Meringues with Walnuts and Oranges 94

My All Time Favorite Fudge Brownies 95

Oatmeal Chocolate Chip
    Cranberry Cookies 96

Old Fashioned Molasses Spice Cookies 98

Orchard Fruit Crumble 99

Pecan Praline Chocolate Cravings 100

Plum Crisp Italian Style 102

Sassy Lemon Cookies 104

The Chosen Chews 105

Yogurt Almond Cake
    with Lemon curd filling 106

Altar Bread 109

Almond Cake with Chamomile

Tea brings a scent of the mysterious to Daniel Patterson's refined, nearly gluten-free cake from Spain. The floral and grassy flavors of chamomile are subtle in this recipe and often leave our guests trying to figure out what the mystery background flavor is. This is not a high-rising cake, but its richness and flavor easily compensate for its stature. If you don't have a stand-up mixer, an electric beater will easily substitute. This cake is lovely served with ripe pear slices. **Yields 10 to 12 servings.**

¼ cup sliced toasted almonds to line the cake pan
4 tablespoons unsalted butter, melted
2 tablespoons wheat or rice flour to dust the cake pan
4 tablespoons chamomile tea leaves
1 cup plus 2 tablespoons sliced almonds
¾ cup sugar
½ teaspoon salt
4 large eggs, 1 separated
Grated zest of 1 lemon
3 tablespoons cornstarch
¼ teaspoon baking powder
Cooking-oil spray
Confectioners' sugar

1. Preheat the oven to 320 degrees. Pour the ¼ cup of almonds onto a baking tin. Bake these in an oven for approximately 6 minutes or until they are slightly brown and become fragrant.

2. Butter a 9-inch cake pan. Coat the inside of the pan with flour and shake off excess. Sprinkle the toasted sliced almonds on the bottom of the pan.

3. In a food processor, grind the tea, the remaining almonds, sugar and a large pinch of salt into a paste. If the mixture is dry, add 1 egg white to form a paste. Otherwise, add the white at the end of the processing.

4. Transfer the almond paste to a stand-up mixer fitted with a paddle attachment. Add 1 yolk and 1 egg and beat on medium-low for 1 minute. Add another egg and beat for another minute. Add the last egg and the lemon zest and beat on medium for 5 minutes.

5. Using as few strokes as possible, fold in the cornstarch and baking powder with a rubber spatula until mostly combined. Pour in the melted butter, a little at a time, folding just until combined. Do not over mix.

6. Pour the batter into the cake pan and bake until the center is just set, about 40 minutes. Let cool for 6 minutes. Grease a cake plate with cooking-oil spray.

Almond Stuffed Poached Pears

Always on the prowl for satisfying, low fat desserts, I discovered these poached pears that cradle a tender almond filling. The pears start in the pot with a gentle simmer and finish in the oven to make a palate-pleasing conclusion to an early fall dinner. While these pears are delicious by themselves, you can accompany them with vanilla ice cream or crunchy biscotti. Why not both?

Yields 6 portions.

Pear Poaching

2½ cups any white or red wine
2½ cups water
⅔ cup granulated sugar
2 tablespoons lemon juice from 1 lemon
 plus 5 long strips of lemon zest
 removed with a vegetable peeler
3 inch piece of cinnamon stick
15 whole black peppercorns
3 whole cloves
⅛ teaspoon salt
½ vanilla bean, slit in half lengthwise
 (optional) or 1 teaspoon vanilla extract
6 softening but still firm pears,
 preferably Bosc
1 tablespoon cornstarch (optional,
 if additional thickening needed)

Pear Filling

½ cup coarsely chopped almonds
1 tablespoon of softened butter
1½ tablespoons packed brown sugar
½ teaspoon ground cinnamon
2 teaspoons unbleached white flour
1 teaspoon almond extract

1. Combine wine, water, sugar, lemon juice and zest, cinnamon, peppercorns, cloves, and salt in large, nonreactive saucepan (not aluminum or cast iron). Scrape seeds from vanilla bean pod (if using), and add seeds and pod to saucepan, or add the vanilla extract. Bring mixture to simmer over medium heat, stirring occasionally to dissolve the sugar.

2. While the poaching liquid warms, peel, halve and core the pears. Slide pears into poaching liquid and simmer covered over very low heat until pears are tender but still firm to the touch, about 6-10 minutes. If unsure, test doneness with a toothpick or skewer. Poaching can be done up to two days ahead of time.

3. Remove the partially cooked pears and set aside. Strain the poaching liquid, bring to a boil, and let reduce until half of the liquid has evaporated. If the liquid is not thick enough to use as a sauce, mix cornstarch with 1 tablespoon of water to make a slurry. Add this slurry to the reduced poaching liquid and briefly bring the pot to a boil. Remove from heat and set aside.

4. Preheat the oven to 350 degrees. Combine the almonds, butter, brown sugar, cinnamon, flour, and almond extract in a small bowl.

5. Place the pears cut side up on a baking pan. Fill the cavities of the pears with the almond stuffing.

6. Bake the pears at 350 degrees for 10 minutes. Baste the pears with the thickened poaching liquid and return to the oven for a final 10 minutes. Serve warm or at room temperature bathed in a small pool of the poaching liquid.

CHOCOLATE GO AHEAD COOKIES

A friend of mine on a diet once told me that she saved her indulgent calories for desserts that were really worth it. To any chocolate lover, I would advise: go-ahead, these are worth it. I love how the tops of these cookies crack, yet the insides remain tender and intensely chocolaty. A good-quality bittersweet chocolate makes these cookies even better. As with most cookies, it's better to slightly underbake these rather than to overbake. Dorie Greenspan created the original version of this recipe in Baking, From My Home To Yours.

Yields 35 cookies.

10 tablespoons butter, cut into 10 pieces (1¼ sticks of butter)
1¼ cups light brown sugar, packed
10 ounces bittersweet chocolate, coarsely chopped
2½ cups all-purpose flour
½ cup unsweetened cocoa
1 teaspoon baking soda
½ teaspoon salt
½ teaspoon ground cinnamon
⅛ teaspoon ground cloves
2 large eggs
2 tablespoons almond, hazelnut, or dried cranberry for optional topping

1. Melt the butter and sugar over low heat in a small saucepan. Add the chocolate and stir until fully melted; the sugar may still be grainy. Transfer this mixture to stand mixer or into a large bowl. Run the mixer on low for 2 minutes to cool the mixture.

2. Sift together the flour, cocoa, baking soda, salt, cinnamon, and cloves.

3. Beat the eggs one at a time into the liquid chocolate. Incorporate the flour mixture, running the mixer on low until the dough becomes smooth and shiny. When stirred, it will clean the sides of the bowl and form a ball.

4. Cut the dough in half. Flatten it with your hands to the size of a paperback book and wrap each piece in plastic wrap. Refrigerate the dough for at least an hour, or as long as 3 days.

5. Position the oven racks to divide the oven into thirds and preheat the oven to 350 degrees. If the dough is extremely firm, let it soften on the counter for 30 minutes before scooping.

6. Grease two baking sheets or line them with parchment or a silicone mat. Depending on the size of your baking sheets, you may need to bake the cookies in batches.

7. Scoop one tablespoon of dough at a time and roll into firm balls. The balls may break, but are easily compacted together. Place the balls about one inch apart on the baking sheets and gently press each one down a bit with your fingers.

8. Place in the oven for five to six minutes. Rotate the baking sheets from top to bottom and front to back, then return to oven for another five to six minutes.

9. When done, the cookies should be soft and delicate in the middle and beginning to crackle across the top. Allow the cookies to rest on the sheets for two minutes before using a spatula to transfer the cookies to a cooling rack.

10. You may choose to garnish the cookies with a piece of dried fruit or nut while the cookies are still soft. Wrapped airtight, the cookies can be kept for about 5 days at room temperature or frozen for up to 2 months.

DEEP DARK CHOCOLATE BUNDT CAKE

Moist and dark as a root cellar, this cake brings together three affable performers: coffee, chocolate, and brandy. Inspired by the Moosewood Restaurant, this exquisite cake has the density of a pudding cake without the undue sweetness. It is elegant with a little powdered sugar, but it really comes into its own with whipped cream and fresh raspberries or strawberries. I have also suggested a chocolate glaze in the final step. The cake batter is very thin and has a long, slow baking time at a low temperature. This cake freezes well if thoroughly wrapped when cooled.

Yields 1 cake (14 to 18 slices).

1 tablespoon butter to grease the pan
1 tablespoon cocoa powder (can also substitute
    instant espresso powder)
1½ cups strong freshly-brewed coffee
¼ cup brandy, bourbon, or a coffee,
    chocolate or mocha liqueur
½ pound (2 sticks) unsalted butter
3 ounces unsweetened (baker's) chocolate
2 cups sugar
4 tablespoons raspberry jam
2 cups cake flour (all-purpose flour
    may be substituted)
¼ teaspoon salt
1 teaspoon baking soda
2 teaspoon vanilla extract
2 large eggs, beaten

1. Preheat oven to 275 degrees. Generously butter a 10-inch Bundt pan. Dust with cocoa.

2. Using a sauce pot with a thick base, heat the coffee, liquor, butter, and chocolate over medium heat until the butter and chocolate have melted. Stir in the sugar and the raspberry jam. Transfer this batter to a large mixer bowl.

3. Beat in the flour, salt, baking soda, and vanilla. Add the eggs and beat until the batter is smooth and evenly colored.

4. Pour the batter into the prepared Bundt pan and bake for about 1½ hours until the cake pulls away from the sides of the pan and the middle springs back when touched.

5. Cool in the pan for 10 minutes. Invert the cake onto a serving plate, leaving the pan in place over the cake until the cake is cool. The cake cuts best when cool.

6. Powdered sugar sprinkled on top just before cutting the cake is handsome. A tastier alternative is to make a glaze with 3 ounces of bittersweet chocolate melted with 2 tablespoons water, coffee, or orange liqueur.

Florentine Bars

A simple orange caramel scrumptiously mingles with sliced almonds on top of this chewy dessert bar. It has an elegant look with a simple preparation. Don't be tempted to touch or taste the caramel until it has thoroughly cooled, because the molten sugar can give you painful burns. If you don't have a candy thermometer you can test the doneness of the sugar mixture the old fashioned way: drop a tiny bit of the caramel into a cup of cold water. The cooled texture of the caramel will reveal its done-ness. (See step 4 below.)

Yields 20 squares.

The Crust

1½ cups unbleached all-purpose flour
1¼ cups quick-cooking oats
⅓ cup granulated sugar
⅓ cup packed light brown sugar
¼ teaspoon baking soda
¼ teaspoon table salt
½ cup finely chopped pecans or almonds,
   or a combination
12 tablespoons unsalted butter (1½ sticks),
   cut into 12 pieces and softened

The Filling

½ cup unsalted butter
⅔ cup granulated sugar
3 tablespoons honey
½ cup heavy cream
2 teaspoons grated orange zest
2 cups sliced almonds

1. THE CRUST: Adjust the oven rack to lower-middle position and heat oven to 350 degrees. Line a 9-inch-square baking pan with foil. (Lining the pan with foil makes removal for cutting very easy.) Spray the foil-lined baking pan with nonstick cooking spray.

2. In the bowl of a standing-mixer, mix flour, oats, sugars, baking soda, salt, and nuts at low speed until combined, about 30 seconds. With mixer running at low speed, add butter pieces. Continue to beat until mixture is well blended and resembles wet sand, about 2 minutes.

3. Transfer the mixture to the prepared pan and use fingers to press the crumbs into a consistent thickness. Bake until barely brown, about 18 minutes.

4. THE FILLING: Combine the butter, sugar, and honey in a heavy-bottomed saucepan. Heat over low heat, stirring occasionally until the sugar is dissolved. Increase the heat to medium and add the cream and the orange zest. Boil the mixture until a candy thermometer reads 250 degrees, or until a small sample, when dropped in cold water, forms a cohesive, gum-like, soft ball. Working quickly, add the sliced almonds and stir thoroughly.

5. Spread the nut mixture evenly over the prebaked crust. Bake until the nut mixture has leveled out and gently bubbles around the sides, about 10 minutes.

6. Cool for about two hours on a wire rack to room temperature, then flip the pan, remove the foil and transfer to a cutting board. Cut into 1¼- to 1½-inch squares and serve. If well wrapped, these bars will store in the freezer for up to one month.

Full-of-Fruit Bars

Everbody knows about moderation, but in our dining room there are rarely any of these addictive bars left over. The fruits and nuts let this bar be many things at once: chewy, crunchy, sour, sweet … maybe just one more bar to eat. Many thanks to the King Arthur Flour bakers for their creativity.
Yields 16 bars.

The Crust

8 tablespoons (1 stick) unsalted butter,
   cut into small pieces
½ cup confectioners' sugar
¼ teaspoon salt
2 teaspoons vanilla extract
1¼ cups all-purpose flour

The Topping

4 tablespoons unsalted butter
¼ teaspoon salt
½ cup granulated sugar
½ cup half-and-half
1½ cups of almost any dried fruit, cut into pea size
   pieces: cranberries, apricots, cherries, pineapple,
   mango, pear, and apple are all good choices. Raisins
   tend to blacken, so are best avoided.
1 cup diced pecans
1 tablespoon lemon juice

1. Preheat the oven to 375 degrees. Lightly grease a 9-inch by 9-inch pan.

2. Using a standing-mixer beat together the butter, sugar, salt, and vanilla.

3. Add the flour, scraping the bowl and mixing until everything is well combined with the texture of thick cornmeal.

4. Press the crust into the bottom of the prepared pan and bake for 12 to 14 minutes, until lightly browned.

5. For the topping, melt the butter in a small saucepan with the salt, sugar, and half-and-half. Bring the mixture to a boil. Boil for 5 minutes, stirring constantly, until the mixture thickens slightly. Turn off the heat and stir in the fruit, nuts, and lemon juice. Spread the topping over the baked crust.

6. Bake the bars for 14 to 16 minutes, until the fruit mixture is bubbly. If baking in a convection oven, cover the pan with foil that does not touch the fruit mixture for the first 10 minutes. Remove the foil and finish baking for an additional 10 minutes.

7. Allow the bars to cool for 45 minutes. Then use a butter knife to loosen the edges of the bars from the pan. Don't wait too long, or they will have cemented themselves to the sides of the pan. Cut the bars when they're completely cool. If wrapped well, these store in the freezer up to one month.

GINGER DREAMS

For those who love the bite of ginger in their sweets, this will be a gratifying treat: a thin, chewy, intensely flavored gingerbread with a crystallized ginger streusel on top. My gratitude to the bakers at King Arthur Flour kitchens who thought to combine these flavors and textures into one of my all-time favorites (and, yes, their flours really are better). Note that crystallized ginger and candied ginger are not the same. Candied ginger is very difficult to cut and not a good substitute.

Yields about 28 squares.

THE SQUARES
1¼ cups all-purpose flour
2 teaspoons ground ginger
1 teaspoon ground allspice
¾ teaspoon salt
¼ teaspoon baking soda
½ cup diced crystallized ginger
¼ cup molasses
2 eggs
1⅓ cups dark brown sugar, firmly packed
¼ cup (½ stick) butter, melted

THE STREUSEL TOPPING
1⅓ cups all-purpose flour
½ cup (1 stick) butter, cut into small pieces
Pinch of salt
¾ cup dark brown sugar, firmly packed
½ cup diced crystallized ginger

1. In a medium-sized mixing bowl, whisk together the flour, ginger, allspice, salt, baking soda, and crystallized ginger.

2. In a separate bowl, stir together the molasses, eggs, brown sugar, and butter.

3. Combine the wet and dry ingredients, beating until smooth. Spread the very thick batter in a lightly greased 13 x 9-inch pan.

4. Bake the squares in a preheated 350 degrees oven for 20 minutes.

5. STREUSEL TOPPING: While the base cooks, make the streusel topping, using a pastry blender, electric mixer, or your fingers. Mix together the flour, butter, salt, and brown sugar until it is fairly well-blended; some chunks of butter can remain. Mix in the crystallized ginger.

6. Sprinkle on the streusel, and bake an additional 25 minutes, until the streusel is a deep, golden brown. Remove the squares from the oven, and run a knife around the edges of the pan to loosen them. Allow them to cool, then cut into 2-inch squares.

HEAVENLY HONEY-SEARED PINEAPPLE

Almost everything we associate with food being golden brown and delicious has to do with caramelizing. In this recipe we enhance the pineapple's natural sugar with honey and lime juice and let the high heat of a grill or sauté pan toast those sugars. The result is a spirited topping for cakes, ice cream, or even teriyaki salmon. Gourmet can be so easy!

Yields 6 servings.

½ cup honey
¼ cup fresh lime juice
1 tablespoon grated lime peel
1 teaspoon orange-flower water*
1 large ripe pineapple
¼ cup minced fresh mint for garnish

*Sold at specialty foods section of supermarkets

1. Whisk first 3 ingredients in large glass baking dish. Add orange flower water, if using.

2. Peel pineapple and cut crosswise into 6 rounds. Cut out the core; discard. Soak the pineapple in the lime and honey; turn to coat. Let the pineapple marinate at room temperature for 1 to 2 hours.

3. Heat a grill to medium heat or heat a sauté pan with a little vegetable oil to medium-high heat. Remove pineapple from marinade and reserve the marinade. Grill or sear the pineapple until golden brown, about 3 minutes per side.

4. Transfer the cooked pineapple to a serving dish. Drizzle the reserved marinade on top of it. Sprinkle with mint.
Serve warm or chilled.

Indian Pudding Cake

When the weather cools, traditional New England Indian pudding is a favorite comfort food of mine. With the help of a few eggs, the pudding becomes a sliceable cake that is gluten-free and every bit as delicious. A little garnish goes a long way with this cake. We have served it with a cinnamon whipped cream or spiced apples, a simple sauce made from dried cranberries, sliced plums, hard sauce, or that old standby, good vanilla ice cream. Adapted with gratitude from Myra Kornfeld's book, The Healthy Hedonist.

Yields 1 cake, about 12 portions.

2½ cups milk
¾ cup polenta or cornmeal
¼ cup molasses, preferably blackstrap
¼ cup maple syrup
¾ cup granulated sugar
1 tablespoon ground cinnamon
½ teaspoon ground nutmeg
1½ teaspoons ground ginger
½ teaspoon salt
1 tablespoon grated orange zest
1 teaspoon vanilla extract
4 eggs, separated

1. Preheat the oven to 350 degrees. Grease a 9-inch spring form pan. Fill a 4-quart saucepan two-thirds with water and bring to a simmer to make a double boiler.

2. In a medium-size bowl, whisk together the milk, polenta, molasses, maple syrup, ¼ cup of the sugar, cinnamon, nutmeg, ginger, and the salt.

3. Set the milk mixture over the simmering water and cover it with foil. Stir the mixture every 5 to 10 minutes. After 40 to 60 minutes the mixture should thicken enough for a spoon to stand vertically in it.

4. Remove the milk mixture from the heat and add the orange zest and vanilla. Add a few ounces of this mixture gradually to the egg yolks to warm them up, then stir in all of the warmed egg yolks into the milk mixture.

5. In a bowl or mixer, whip the egg whites until frothy. Slowly add the remaining ½ cup of sugar and continue beating until the whites are stiff and glossy. Stir a quarter of the beaten egg whites into the polenta and milk mixture to make the batter more supple. Fold in the remaining whites, one-third at a time, until thoroughly combined.

6. Pour the batter into the greased pan and bake about 45 minutes or until a knife inserted in the center of the pan comes out clean. Cool for 15 minutes before releasing the sides of the cake.

MERINGUES WITH WALNUTS & ORANGE

The plain meringue has plenty of sweetness to entice a child, but how about flavors more uncommon to charm the grown-ups? The flavors of orange and walnut make an unexpectedly pleasing duo that makes these rather sweet cookies disappear quickly. This recipe gently warms the egg whites before beating in order to avoid the gritty texture of sugar that has not completely dissolved. All meringues require parchment paper or silicone sheets on your baking pans to prevent sticking. For a thoroughly crunchy bite, let the cookies dry out overnight in a turned-off oven. Humidity is the enemy of meringues, so avoid making these on hot, humid days. My respect and appreciation to Carole Walter, who described this variation in her sensational book, Great Cookies.
Yields about 50 silver dollar-size cookies.

4 large egg whites at room temperature
2½ cups strained confectioners' sugar
1½ teaspoons vanilla extract
4 teaspoons white vinegar
1½ teaspoons grated orange zest
3½ cups broken walnuts (about 11 ounces by weight)

1. Preheat the oven to 225 degrees. Dab the corners of the cookie sheets lightly with oil and then place the parchment on top. This helps hold down the parchment when scooping.

2. Place the egg whites and sugar in the bowl of an electric mixer and stir with a hand whisk. Place the bowl over a saucepan with a couple inches of simmering water. Whisk the mixture lightly but continuously. You will notice the sugar get lumpy at first but it will smooth out as the mixture warms. Stop after about 3 minutes when the mixture reaches 115 to 120 degrees.

3. Remove the bowl from the heat and attach it to an electric mixer. Beat the egg mixture for 4 to 5 minutes on medium-high speed with a whip attachment. The mixture should form a thick meringue.

4. Reduce the speed to medium and add the vanilla, vinegar, and orange zest. Mix just until these items are incorporated. Don't worry if the meringue does not stand up in firm peaks.

5. Remove the bowl from the machine and fold in the walnut pieces with a rubber spatula.

6. Using a tablespoon, drop silver-dollar-size portions of meringue onto lined cookie sheets. You may need to frequently stir the mixture because the walnuts will sink towards the bottom. Meringues should be about 1½ inches apart.

7. Bake the meringues for 45 minutes at 225 degrees. Rotate the cookie tins to prevent the cookies from browning and return them to the oven. After 30 minutes turn the oven off and let the cookies sit at least 3 hours or overnight.

My All-Time Favorite Fudge Brownies

Chocolaty, fudgy, surprisingly quick to make, Molly Katzen created this recipe in her influential book The Moosewood Cookbook *more than 30 years ago. I have added the walnut pieces and offer a few alternatives if you want to try to build upon near perfection. This is a good opportunity to make use of a high-quality chocolate if available. These freeze well if thoroughly wrapped when cooled.*

Yields about 24 brownies.

½ cup butter, cut into pieces
3 ounces unsweetened chocolate
1 cup lightly packed brown sugar
½ teaspoon pure vanilla extract
2 eggs, lightly beaten
½ cup unbleached all-purpose flour
1½ cups walnut pieces

1. Preheat the oven to 350 degrees. Grease an 8- or 9-inch square baking pan. Create a double boiler on the stove by adding two inches of water to a pot and bring it to a simmer.

2. Melt butter and chocolate together in the double boiler on low heat. When melted, remove from heat.

3. Add the sugar and vanilla and beat with a whisk. Add the eggs and continue to beat well. Stir in flour and mix until smooth. Fold one cup of the walnuts into the batter.

4. Pour batter into prepared baking pan. Sprinkle the last ½ cup of the walnuts on top of the batter. Bake for about twenty minutes or until the brownies begin to pull away from the sides of the pan, but are still fudgy in the center. Bake an additional five minutes if you prefer cake-like brownies.

Options: Add any of these to the batter for worthy variations: half a banana, mashed, or 2 to 4 tablespoons of strong black coffee or espresso powder, or 1 teaspoon grated fresh orange rind, or ½ teaspoon allspice or cinnamon.

Oatmeal Chocolate Chip Cranberry Cookies

Why is it that we make huge batches of this cookie dough to freeze and just can't ever seem to have enough? This hybrid of a cookie delights the inner cookie monster of every sort. There are oats and cranberries for chewiness and the suggestion of health (let's be clear: they are cookies, not nutrition bars), creamy chocolate for those who wish that every cookie should be a chocolate chip cookie, and finally, toasted pecans for their savory flavor and crunchy bite. With a soft center and crisp surface, these cookies are the gold standard of sweet treats. Our version of these treasures was inspired by Cooks Illustrated.
Yields sixteen 4-inch cookies.

1 cup pecans
½ teaspoon salt
1¼ cups all-purpose flour
¾ teaspoon baking powder
½ teaspoon baking soda
½ teaspoon table salt
1¼ cups old-fashioned rolled oats
1 cup dried cranberries, coarsely chopped
¾ cup bittersweet chocolate chips (may substitute semi-sweet)
1½ sticks unsalted butter, softened but still cool
1¼ cups packed dark brown sugar
¼ cup granulated sugar
1 large egg
1 teaspoon vanilla extract

1. Preheat oven to 350 degrees. Toast the pecans by laying them out on a cookie sheet. Sprinkle with salt and roast in a 350 degree oven until slightly darkened, about 5 to 7 minutes. Coarsely chop the pecans.

2. Prepare cookie tins by greasing or lining with parchment paper.

3. In a medium bowl stir together flour, baking powder, baking soda, and salt. In second medium bowl, stir together oats, pecans, cranberries, and chocolate chips.

4. In standing mixer beat together the butter and both sugars at medium speed until no sugar lumps remain. Scrape down the sides of the bowl with a rubber spatula. Add the egg and vanilla and beat until fully incorporated.

5. From this point on the goal is to run the mixer as little as possible, using it just enough to incorporate the ingredients. Add the flour mixture and then scrape the bowl down with the spatula. Gradually add the oat/nut mixture and give the dough a final stir with the spatula. For best results, refrigerate the dough for 1 hour before portioning.

6. Scoop the dough into ping-pong ball size portions. Place the balls about 2½ inches apart on the cookie tin and gently press to 1-inch thickness.

7. If possible, avoid using the top shelf of the oven when baking. Bake for 12 minutes, then rotate the pans. After a final 8 to 10 minutes in the oven the cookies will be medium brown and edges will begin to set. The centers will be very soft and appear under done, but this is the time to remove them from the oven.

8. After the cookies cool for 5 minutes use a spatula to transfer cookies to a wire rack and cool to room temperature. Here comes the yummy part.

Clockwise from Left:

Sassy Lemon Cookies

Full of Fruit Bars

Oatmeal Chocolate Chip
Cranberry Cookies

Chocolate Go Ahead Cookies

OLD FASHIONED MOLASSES SPICE COOKIES

If you find me eating these delectable cookies with a homemade applesauce, you will know that I am lingering just short of heaven. These cookies are vastly better when soft and chewy rather than dry and crackly, which over-baking will quickly achieve. Expect that the cookies should look slightly raw and under-baked when you remove them from the oven.

Yields about 22 cookies.

⅓ cup granulated sugar, plus ½ cup for dipping
2¼ cups unbleached all-purpose flour
1 teaspoon baking soda
1 tablespoon ground cinnamon
1 tablespoon ground ginger
1 teaspoon ground cloves
½ teaspoon ground allspice
⅓ teaspoon ground black pepper
¼ teaspoon table salt
1½ sticks unsalted butter, softened
⅓ cup packed dark brown sugar
1 large egg yolk
1 teaspoon vanilla extract
½ cup molasses, light or dark

1. Adjust oven rack to middle position and preheat oven to 375 degrees. Prepare two baking sheets with grease, parchment paper, or silicone mats. Pour ½ cup of sugar into a small bowl to roll the cookie dough in.

2. Whisk flour, baking soda, spices, pepper, and salt in medium bowl until thoroughly combined; set aside.

3. In standing mixer fitted with paddle attachment, beat butter with brown sugar and remaining granulated sugar at medium-high speed until light and fluffy, about 3 minutes.

4. Reduce speed to medium-low and add yolk and vanilla. Increase speed to medium and beat until incorporated, about 20 seconds. Reduce speed to medium-low and add molasses. Scrape the bottom and sides of bowl with a rubber spatula to make sure the ingredients are thoroughly mixed.

5. Reduce speed to lowest setting. Add flour mixture and beat until just incorporated, about 30 seconds, scraping bowl down once. Give dough a final stir with rubber spatula to ensure that no pockets of flour remain at bottom. Dough will be soft.

6. Using a tablespoon measure, scoop a heaping tablespoon of dough and roll between palms into a one-and-a-half-inch ball, then roll that in the bowl of sugar. Repeat with remaining dough. Press the balls onto the prepared baking sheet to slightly flatten them, spacing them about 2 inches apart. If your hands get sticky, moisten them with a little water.

7. Bake about 6 minutes, then rotate baking sheet. Bake an additional 5 minutes, until cookies are browned, but still puffy, and edges have begun to set but centers are still soft. Cookies will look raw between the cracks and seem underdone.

8. Cool cookies to room temperature and enjoy! If stored in an airtight container these cookies will be delicious up to five days.

ORCHARD FRUIT CRUMBLE

I admire versatility in a recipe. A good fruit crisp adapts to most any seasonal fruit, but in this case the recipe makes use of peaches when there may not be any fresh ones available. When you can't find fresh peaches, then frozen peaches come to the rescue. Here, we cook them slightly, add peach jam to intensify the flavor, and then finish with a unique crunchy cornmeal and walnut topping. Whether you choose to use peaches, blueberries, thin sliced apples, or even strawberry-rhubarb, don't forget to serve the whipped cream or the ice cream that slowly melts into the hot filling with delicious abandon. The crumb topping can be made ahead of time; just cover and chill it until ready to bake. **Yields 4 portions.**

THE TOPPING

½ cup unbleached white flour
½ cup cornmeal (¼ cup medium grind and
   ¼ cup coarse-ground if possible)
⅓ cup white sugar
¼ teaspoon salt
⅓ cup cold butter (⅔ of a stick),
   cut into kidney bean size pieces
2 tablespoons chopped toasted walnuts

THE FRUIT FILLING

1 pound frozen but thawed sliced fresh peaches
   (3 cups fresh, peeled)
⅓ cup sugar
⅓ cup peach jam or preserves
½ teaspoon ground cinnamon
1 tablespoon fresh lemon juice

1. Preheat the oven to 375 degrees.

2. In a food processor, mix the flour, cornmeal, sugar, and salt. Add the chilled pieces of butter. Pulse until the dough has the texture of wet sand. Alternately, in a mixing bowl you can cut the butter into the mixture with two knives until coarse crumbs form. Stir in the walnuts and refrigerate until needed.

3. Combine the peaches, sugar, preserves and cinnamon in a small pot and warm gently for about 5 minutes. This will soften the peaches, which are often picked before ripeness. Turn off the heat and add the lemon juice.

4. Spread the fruit mixture in an ungreased 9- or 10-inch pie pan. Sprinkle the topping mixture evenly over the fruit. Bake until the fruit is bubbling and the topping is golden, about 30 minutes. Serve warm or at room temperature with your favorite creamy indulgence.

Pecan Praline Chocolate Cravings

I'll be frank: these are so good that once tasted, the experience of eating these returns like a puppy ready to play. You could call it a harmony of flavors or a symbiotic relationship of chocolate to roasted nuts that balances like an elegantly written equation. Praline and chocolate have that ability and leave one craving the sensation long after they are gone. Once cooled, these have a chewy, dense, chocolate brownie on the bottom and butterscotchy pecans with a crunchy caramelized crust on top. Gratefully adapted from Alice Medrich's superb book, Chewy Gooey Crispy Crunchy.

Yields 24 to 30 bars

Brownie Layer

4 ounces unsweetened chocolate,
   cut into pieces for melting
1 stick unsalted butter
1 cup plus 2 tablespoons sugar
1½ teaspoon vanilla extract
¼ teaspoon salt
2 large eggs, beaten
½ cup all-purpose flour
2 teaspoons unsweetened cocoa powder
   or espresso powder

Pecan Topping

½ cup all-purpose flour
½ teaspoon baking soda
½ teaspoon cinnamon
8 tablespoons unsalted butter, melted
¾ cup packed brown sugar
½ teaspoon salt
2 large egg yolks
1 teaspoon vanilla extract
2½ cups coarsely chopped pecans
   or walnuts (8.75 ounce)

1. THE BROWNIE LAYER: Preheat oven to 350 degrees. Line the bottom and sides of a 9 x 13 inch baking pan with foil and lightly oil it. Start a saucepan simmering with water for the double boiler.

2. Place chopped chocolate and butter in a metal bowl over the pot of simmering water and allow chocolate to melt. Stir until completely melted and smooth. Remove from heat.

3. Stir in sugar, vanilla, and salt with a wooden spoon.

4. Add the eggs and mix well.

5. Add in the flour and the cocoa or espresso powder and beat vigorously until batter is smooth and glossy and begins to come away from the sides of the pan.

6. Scrape batter into the prepared pan and set aside.

7. PECAN TOPPING: Combine flour, baking soda, and cinnamon in a small bowl and mix well using a fork.

8. In a separate bowl combine the melted butter with the brown sugar and salt.

9. Add in the egg yolks and vanilla.

10. Add the flour mixture followed by the pecans; mix well.

11. Drop by spoonfuls on top of the brownie layer. Spread and cover the brownie layer with the topping.

12. Bake for 15 minutes, then rotate the pan in the oven for even cooking. Bake a final 5 to 10 minutes or until the top is completely brown and cracked.

13. Allow to cool completely on a wire rack. Remove by turning the entire pan upside down onto a cutting board and pulling off the foil. The bars are ready to cut. Turn them right-side up and they are ready to enjoy.

Plum Crisp Italian Style

Plums, whether fresh or dried, are too often deprived of the attention they deserve. In my kitchen they have found their way into Moroccan stews and beef sauces and perhaps best of all, into this dessert, where they are used to marvelous ends. Prune plums have a brief late summer season, and are around for only a few weeks in the early fall. When baked, they're sweet, sticky, and jammy. Cinnamon and cardamom enhance the wine-like flavors that develop inside cooked plums. This topping is a little richer than the Orchard Fruit Crumble topping and makes a nice contrast to the plums that bubble away beneath.
Yields 8 to 10 servings.

1 cup all-purpose flour
¼ cup whole wheat flour
⅓ cup plus 1 tablespoon finely chopped walnuts
½ cup granulated sugar, divided into 2 equal portions
¼ cup firmly packed dark brown sugar
¼ teaspoon ground cinnamon
⅛ teaspoon ground cardamom
½ cup (1 stick) unsalted butter, melted and
    cooled to room temperature
2¼ pounds Italian prune plums,
    pitted and quartered (6 cups)
¼ teaspoon nutmeg
1 tablespoon lemon juice

1. Preheat the oven to 375 degrees.

2. In a large bowl, whisk together both flours, walnuts, ¼ cup granulated sugar, the brown sugar, cinnamon, and cardamom.

3. Slowly drizzle in the butter and combine with a fork until the mixture is crumbly. Break up any large crumbs with your fingers. The crumbs should be smaller than 1 inch in size (otherwise they won't cook all the way through).

4. In another large bowl, combine the plums, the remaining ¼ cup of granulated sugar, the nutmeg, and lemon juice (unless the plums are naturally tart). Toss well. Spoon the fruit into a buttered 2-quart gratin or shallow casserole dish. Sprinkle the crumbs evenly on top of the fruit.

5. Bake the crisp until the fruit is bubbling and the topping browned, 50 to 55 minutes. Serve hot or warm.

Sassy Lemon Cookies

Carole Walter, the creator of these lip-smacking cookies, once mentioned that while some foods lavish us with vitamins and minerals, others nourish us with pleasure. All things in moderation, except, perhaps, the lemon that pervades these tender butter cookies with abandon.
Yields 32 cookies.

2¾ cup all purpose flour
1 teaspoon cream of tartar
½ teaspoon baking soda
⅓ teaspoon salt
1 cup (2 sticks) unsalted butter,
    slightly firm and cut into small pieces
2 tablespoons freshly grated lemon zest
1½ cups sugar
4 large egg yolks
¼ cup fresh lemon juice
1 teaspoon pure vanilla extract

The Glaze
1 teaspoon vanilla extract
¼ cup fresh lemon juice
Zest of one lemon
1½ cups powdered sugar

1. Preheat the oven to 350 degrees. Prepare two baking sheets with grease, parchment paper, or silicone mats.

2. Sift together the flour, cream of tartar, baking soda, and salt. Sifting twice will create a lighter cookie.

3. Using an electric mixer fitted with a paddle attachment, mix the butter with the lemon zest until creamy and lightened in color, about 2 minutes. Add the sugar in a steady stream, until fully incorporated. Blend in the egg yolks, mix for another minute, then pour in the lemon juice and the vanilla, scraping down the bowl as needed.

4. Reduce the mixer speed to low and add the dry ingredients in three additions, mixing just until blended. Transfer the dough to a clean bowl, cover with plastic wrap, and chill for one hour.

5. Scoop the dough into rounds a little smaller than a ping-pong ball. Place the balls on cookie sheets 2 inches apart. Slightly flatten the balls with the heels of your hand. Putting some flour on your hands will make the dough easier to work with.

6. While the cookies bake, prepare the simple glaze. Whisk together the vanilla, lemon juice, and zest, followed by the powdered sugar. Stir until smooth.

7. Bake the cookies for approximately 8 minutes, then rotate which shelves the pans are cooking on and return to bake for a final seven minutes, or until the edges are golden brown. Allow the cookies to stand for five minutes before using a spatula to transfer them to a cooling rack.

8. Before the cookies cool completely, brush the glaze on each cookie. The glaze will firm up shortly thereafter.

THE CHOSEN CHEWS

Two layers and two textures; it's the double happiness winner of comfort desserts known to make kids squirm and plead for a second piece. The classic combination of brown sugar, coconut, and nuts make these chewy bars irresistible. Inspired by The Baking Sheet Newsletter *from King Arthur's Flour, this version, like Proust's madeleines, makes up part of my own "involuntary memory" of things past.*

Yields about 24 bars.

THE COOKIE LAYER

1 cup unbleached all-purpose flour
½ cup dark brown sugar
1 cup corn flakes
¼ teaspoon salt (omit if using salted butter)
½ cup or 1 stick of unsalted butter
1 teaspoon of vanilla

THE TOPPING

1½ cups packed dark brown sugar
1 tablespoon unbleached all-purpose flour
¼ teaspoon baking powder
2 large eggs, well-beaten
¼ cup honey
1 cup shredded coconut, unsweetened is preferable
1 cup diced nuts: walnuts, pecans, hazelnuts,
   or your favorite nut

1. THE BOTTOM COOKIE LAYER: Preheat oven to 300 degrees and lightly grease a 9 x 13 inch pan.

2. Process the flour, sugar, cornflakes, and salt in a food processor until the flakes are coarsely ground, about 10 seconds. Add the butter and vanilla, then pulse until the mixture resembles coarse meal.

3. Press the mixture firmly into the pan. Bake this for about 10 minutes or until golden brown. Cool on a wire rack for 20 minutes.

4. THE TOPPING: Increase the oven temperature to 325 degrees.

5. In a medium-sized mixing bowl, combine the brown sugar, flour, and baking powder.

6. Pour in the beaten eggs and honey, stirring until smooth. Add the coconut and nuts, mixing until thoroughly combined.

7. Spread dollops of the topping onto the cookie layer. Wet your fingers and spread the topping as evenly as possible.

8. Bake the bars for 30 minutes, until golden brown. Wait to cut until completely cool.

YOGURT ALMOND CAKE with Lemon Curd Filling

Dorie Greenspan described this cake in her book Baking, From My Home To Yours, *and I love it because depending on how you accessorize this, it can play casual or elegant. The lemon curd really is just gilding the lily because this simple cake is versatile enough to eat with just a sprinkle of powdered sugar on top. This cake can be baked in a 9 inch round springform pan or an 8 x 4 inch loaf pan. The round pan makes a more elegant presentation. The original recipe calls for a marmalade or jam glaze but the cake is equally good* au naturel *with toppings of fresh berries, peaches, or plums.*
Note: *if you make the lemon curd filling it will need at least 2 hours to set up before it is cool enough to use. A delicious filling can also be made by mixing raspberry jam with non-dairy whipped topping; it's a bit of a cheat but it tastes great.* **Makes one 9 inch cake round.**

THE CAKE

1 cup all-purpose flour
½ cup ground almonds (or if you have no almonds, use an additional ½ cup of flour)
2 teaspoons baking powder
Pinch salt
1 cup sugar
Zest of 1 lemon
½ cup plain yogurt
3 large eggs
¼ teaspoon vanilla
½ cup light-flavored oil, like canola or soy oil

1. MAKE THE CAKE: Grind the almonds in a food processor with a regular S-shaped chopping blade. Just add a little bit of the sugar to keep the almonds from becoming mushy.

2. Preheat the oven to 350 degrees and lightly grease a 9 inch springform pan.

3. Mix together the flour, ground almonds, baking powder, and salt.

4. In a separate medium bowl, rub the sugar together with the zest to help incorporate the flavor of the natural lemon oil. Whisk the yogurt, eggs, and vanilla into the sugar.

5. Whisk the flour mixture in until just blended. Fold in the oil with a rubber spatula.

6. Scrape the batter into the pan. A round springform pan will take 35-45 minutes while a loaf pan will take 50-55 minutes to bake. The cake is done when it pulls away from the sides of the pan and a toothpick inserted in the center comes out dry.

7. Let the cake cool on a rack for 5 minutes, and then remove it from the pan to continue cooling. Without the filling, the cake will last for 3 days at room temperature if wrapped well. If unglazed, the cake can be frozen for up to 2 months if wrapped very well.

The Lemon Curd

⅓ cup lemon juice, about 2 lemons
2 large eggs
1 egg yolk
½ cup sugar
3 tablespoons unsalted butter,
  cut into ½-inch cubes and chilled
½ teaspoon vanilla extract
Pinch table salt

1. MAKE THE LEMON CURD: Heat lemon juice in small nonreactive saucepan (not aluminum or cast iron) over medium heat until steaming. Do not let it boil.

2. Whisk eggs and yolk in medium nonreactive bowl; gradually whisk in sugar.

3. Whisking constantly, slowly pour hot lemon juice into eggs, then return mixture to saucepan and cook over medium heat, stirring constantly with wooden spoon, until mixture reaches 170 degrees and is thick enough to cling to a spoon, about 3 minutes.

4. Immediately remove pan from heat and stir in cold butter until incorporated; stir in vanilla and salt, then pour curd through fine-mesh strainer into a small nonreactive bowl. Once chilled, the lemon curd can be easily spread between the cake layers.

Altar Bread

Often requested, I am including this recipe nearly verbatim as described by The Monastery of St. John the Evangelist in Cambridge, Massachusetts.
Yields about 16 large (6 inch diameter loaves) or 26 medium (3 inch diameter) loaves.

8 cups whole-wheat flour
8 teaspoons baking powder
4 teaspoons salt
1 cup milk
1 cup oil (vegetable, canola,
    or other light oil)
1 cup water
16 ounces honey
    (1 pound by weight or 1 small jar)

Some advice for bakers beyond the monastery:

"Before you forge ahead to make the loaves to be used on the altar for Easter morning when the Bishop is there and the sanctuary is full: practice! Besides, the birds will find your 'practice runs' to be a special treat!"

"Finally, remember that these aren't just any loaves, but rather they will be made sacred when they are consecrated at the Eucharist. As you go along, take the time to notice the smells, textures, and colors of the dough and loaves. The process of preparing them is both mundane and holy and it involves all your senses. It is a very special way of sharing in the liturgical and spiritual life of your community."

1. Preheat oven to 400 degrees. Sift together the whole-wheat flour, baking powder, and salt into a large bowl.

2. Mix together the milk, oil, water, and honey.

3. Pour liquid into dry ingredients and mix until thoroughly blended; dough should be stiff and moist, and a little sticky.

4. Turn out onto lightly floured board and knead briefly, using additional flour as necessary. For ease of handling, divide into two to four portions and work one at a time. Roll out on lightly floured board about ¼ inch thick. Rolling the dough to a consistent, even thickness will give the best results.

5. Cut into rounds of appropriate size (no larger than 6 ½ inch diameter). Stamp firmly with floured mold or incise with cross, using a sharp, thin knife dipped in cool water. For best results don't incise the cross too deeply or drag the knife across the dough; rather lay it on top and lightly imprint the dough with the knife.

6. Place on a heavy, light-colored, oiled cookie sheet and bake for 12 to 14 minutes, depending on your oven. If you don't have a heavy cookie sheet or an "Airbake" pan, then stack two pans together. The goal in baking is to get a lightly golden brown top, but not toasted. You should find that once the bread has cooled and you break it apart, it is moist and slightly sweet inside.

7. Cool loaves completely before storing them. Wrap well before freezing. May be reheated in microwave—ever so briefly to avoid drying—before use. The loaves can be frozen in tightly sealed containers (such as Ziploc freezer bags) well in advance. Allow 24 hours for them to defrost so that they are room temperature at the time of the service.

INDEX

A

Adam Segal 6
Adelynrood 6, 9
Almond 20, 40, 42, 48, 58, 84, 85, 89, 106
Almond Cake with Chamomile 84
Almond Stuffed Poached Pears 85
Altar Bread 109
Anchovy 29, 52
Apple 13, 40, 43, 48, 71, 72
Apple Cider 71
Apricot 26, 58
Arugula 29
Asian 30, 35, 47, 68
Asparagus 19, 30
Avocado 18, 19, 70

B

Bacon 18
Barley 21
Bars 89, 90, 91, 95, 105
Basil, fresh 32, 48, 78
Beans 24, 41, 44, 62, 64
Beef 73, 74
Beets 32
Bread Crumbs 55, 68, 73, 80, 81
Breakfast/Brunch 12, 13, 15
Buttermilk 12, 36

C

Cabbage 21, 30, 32, 47
Cakes 84, 88, 93, 106
Cancun Shrimp, Avocado & Corn Salad 18

Capers 20, 29, 52, 58
Carrot 13, 21, 25, 40, 41, 62, 67, 71, 75
Chamomile 84
Chapel Garden Salad 19
Chard 24
Charmoula the Great 69
Cheddar, Pear & Ham Sandwich 50
Cheese 29, 32, 36, 38, 50, 54, 78, 81
Chicken 18, 35, 44, 47, 58, 60, 62, 64, 67
Chicken Baja Dilla 58
Chicken Broth 35, 41, 44, 47, 48, 60, 62, 64, 67, 75
Chicken Salad in the Spanish Style 20
Chicken Soup, Vietnamese-Style 47
Chocolate 86, 88, 95, 100
Chocolate Go Ahead Cookies 86
Chosen Chews, The 105
Cider-Brined Pork Chops 71
Cilantro 18, 25, 35, 43, 44, 47, 60, 62, 64, 68, 69
Coconut 13, 105
Coffee 88, 100
Colicchio, Tom 50
Companions. *See Society of the Companions of the Holy Cross*
Cookies 86, 94, 96, 98, 100, 104
Corn 12, 18, 30, 36, 44
Cornmeal Crunch Chicken with Salsa Verde 60
Couscous 26
Cranberry 26, 40, 42, 90, 96
Creamtea 36
Crimson Plum Soup 42

Cucumber 36, 43
Curried Barley Salad 21
Curry 21

D

Dairy-free 18–31, 33, 35, 40, 47, 43–49, 58–73, 79, 80, 92, 94
D'Avila-Latourrette, Brother 19
Deep Dark Chocolate Bundt Cake 88
Deli Thins 50
Dill 54, 75
Distinctive Zucchini Walnut Bread 15

E

Edamame (Soy Beans) 21, 30
Egg 12, 15, 19, 54, 55, 60, 68, 73, 81, 84, 86, 88, 91, 93, 94, 95, 96, 98, 100, 104, 105, 106
Eggplant 35, 70, 78
Eggplant Stacks 78
Emerald Gazpacho 43
English, Todd 29
Escabeche-Style Trout with Tomato Relish 70

F

Fennel 69
Festive Rice Salad 22
Fish 19, 69, 70
Florentine Bars 89
French Pizza: Pissaladière 52
Fresh Chili Chicken Chili 44
Fresh Corn Griddle Cakes 12

Fresh Peach Salsa 79
Full-of-Fruit Bars 90

G

Gentle Gigandes: A Bean Salad 24
Gezer Chai: Moroccan Carrot Salad 25
Ginger 21, 30, 33, 35, 42, 43, 47, 68, 74, 79,
      91, 93, 98
Ginger Dreams 91
Ginger Glazed Pork with Middle Eastern
      Spice Rub 72
Gluten Free 18, 20, 22, 25, 32, 33, 36–44, 41,
      47, 58, 60, 62, 64, 67, 69, 71, 72, 78,
      79, 84, 92, 93
Grapes 43
Greek 24
Green Beans 38
Greenspan, Dorie 86, 106

H

Ham 50
Harvest Couscous Salad 26
Heavenly Honey-Seared Pineapple 92
Henderson, Sabrina 15

I

Indian Pudding Cake 93
Israeli 26

J

Jue, Joyce 35

K

Kalamata Spaghetti Salad 29
Kale 41, 64
Katzen, Molly 54
Ketchup 73
King Arthur Flour 90, 91, 105
Kornfeld, Myra 69, 93

L

Lahey, Jim 52
Lamb 75
Leek 48, 64
Lemon 15, 19, 22, 25, 40, 42, 54, 69, 74, 75,
      84, 85, 90, 99, 102, 104, 106
Lime 18, 22, 33, 43, 44, 47, 60, 64, 74, 79, 92
Low Carb 19, 20, 25, 32, 42, 43, 69, 70, 78,
      79, 81
Low Fat 18–34, 36–44, 47, 52, 69, 70, 72, 78,
      79, 81, 92, 93, 94
Lukins and Rosso 43
Luscious Lentil Soup with Kale 41

M

Maple 93
Marks, Gil 25
McKinstry, Pam 13
Mediterranean 24, 25, 29, 38, 41, 52, 89
Medrich, Alice 100
Melon 43
Meringues with Walnuts & Orange 94
Middle Eastern 25, 62, 69, 72, 74, 80
Molasses 91, 93, 98

Monastery of St. John the Evangelist 109
Moosewood Restaurant 88
Moroccan Chicken & Vegetable Stew 62
Muffins 13
Muhammara Dip 80
Mushrooms 19, 55
My All-Time Favorite Fudge Brownies 95

N

Nut-free 12, 18, 21, 22, 24, 25, 29, 30, 32, 36,
      38, 41, 42, 43, 47, 52, 54, 62, 64, 67,
      68, 69, 70, 71, 72, 73, 74, 75, 79, 88,
      92, 98, 104, 109

O

Oatmeal Chocolate Chip Cranberry Cookies 96
Oats 89, 96
Olives 20, 29, 52, 58, 69
Orange 40, 67, 89, 93, 94
Orchard Fruit Crumble 99
Ortuzar, Sisha 50
Orzo Salad with Chinese Accent 30
Our Mini Meatloaves 73

P

Pam's Morning Glory Muffins 13
Parsley 22, 25, 38, 58, 62, 67, 69, 73, 81
Pasta 29, 30, 35, 47
Patterson, Daniel 84
Peach 79, 99
Peanuts 35, 47
Pear 50, 85

Peas 75, *See also Snow Pea*
Pecan 26, 89, 90, 96, 100
Pecan Praline Chocolate Cravings 100
Peppers 18, 25, 30, 33, 35, 36, 38, 40, 43, 44,
       58, 62, 67, 79, 80
Pineapple 13, 21, 68, 92
Pissaladière: A French Pizza 52
Plum 42, 102
Plum Crisp Italian Style 102
Plum Sauce 72
Pomegranate Molasses 80
Pork 71, 72
Porter, Cole 40
Potato 38, 48
Potato-Leek Soup Goes Green 48
Preface 6
Prune 58, 62
Pumpkin Seed 60

R

Radish 32
Raisin 13, 40, 62
Raspberry 88
Rice 22, 40
   How to Cook 22
   Wild Rice 26, 40
Roast Beet & Watermelon Salad 32
Roasted Red Peppers 20
Roast Sweet Potato Crunch Salad 33
Rosemary & Orange Braised Chicken 67

S

Salads
   with Beans 24
   with Grains 21, 22, 36, 40
   with Potatoes 33, 38
Sandwich 18, 50, 55
Sassy Lemon Cookies 104
Scallion Meatballs with Pineapple-Ginger Glaze 68
SCHC. *See Society of the Companions*
      of the Holy Cross
Seekh Kebab 74
Sesame Oil 30, 35, 68
Shelburne Farms 75
Shrimp 18
Snow, Constance 33
Snow Pea 35
Society of the Companions of the Holy Cross 9
Soups
   Cold 42, 43
   Hot 41, 44, 47, 48
Sour Cream 42, 75
Southwestern 18, 44, 60
Spach, C.D. 12
Spain/Spanish 20, 43, 58, 84
Spinach 19, 48, 54
Spinach Pie with Feta and Dill 54
Spring Lamb Stew with Dill 75
Stuffed Zucchini Boats 81
Summer Chicken Stew with Sweet Corn,
      Tomatoes & Kale 64
Summer Delight Chinese Noodle Salad 35
Sweet Corn Salad with Buttermilk Dressing 36
Sweet Potato 33

T

Tardiff, Pam 13
Tomatillo 60
Tomato 19, 29, 41, 62, 64, 67, 69, 70, 78, 80
Turkey 55, 68
Turkey Mushroom Burger 55
Turnip 62
Tuscan Potato Salad 38

V

Vegetarian 12, 13, 15, 21, 22, 25, 26, 30, 32, 36,
      38, 40, 42, 43, 54, 78, 79, 80, 81, 84

W

Walnuts 13, 15, 50, 80, 94, 95, 99, 102, 105
Walter, Carole 94, 104
Water Chestnut 68
Watermelon 32
Wild Rice. *See Rice*
Wild Waldorf with a Twist 40
Wine 41, 58, 75

Y

Yeast 52
Yogurt 36, 74, 106
Yogurt Almond Cake with Lemon Curd Filling 106

Z

Zucchini 15, 22, 62, 67, 81